GENERAL EDITOR: JAMES GIBSON

JANE AUSTEN	*Emma* Norman Page
	Sense and Sensibility Judy Simons
	Persuasion Judy Simons
	Pride and Prejudice Raymond Wilson
	Mansfield Park Richard Wirdnam
SAMUEL BECKETT	*Waiting for Godot* Jennifer Birkett
WILLIAM BLAKE	*Songs of Innocence and Songs of Experience* Alan Tomlinson
ROBERT BOLT	*A Man for All Seasons* Leonard Smith
CHARLOTTE BRONTË	*Jane Eyre* Robert Miles
EMILY BRONTË	*Wuthering Heights* Hilda D. Spear
JOHN BUNYAN	*The Pilgrim's Progress* Beatrice Batson
GEOFFREY CHAUCER	*The Miller's Tale* Michael Alexander
	The Pardoner's Tale Geoffrey Lester
	The Wife of Bath's Tale Nicholas Marsh
	The Knight's Tale Anne Samson
	The Prologue to the Canterbury Tales Nigel Thomas and Richard Swan
JOSEPH CONRAD	*The Secret Agent* Andrew Mayne
CHARLES DICKENS	*Bleak House* Dennis Butts
	Great Expectations Dennis Butts
	Hard Times Norman Page
GEORGE ELIOT	*Middlemarch* Graham Handley
	Silas Marner Graham Handley
	The Mill on the Floss Helen Wheeler
T. S. ELIOT	*Selected Poems* Andrew Swarbrick
HENRY FIELDING	*Joseph Andrews* Trevor Johnson
E. M. FORSTER	*A Passage to India* Hilda D. Spear
	Howards End Ian Milligan
WILLIAM GOLDING	*The Spire* Rosemary Sumner
	Lord of the Flies Raymond Wilson
OLIVER GOLDSMITH	*She Stoops to Conquer* Paul Ranger
THOMAS HARDY	*The Mayor of Casterbridge* Ray Evans
	Tess of the d'Urbervilles James Gibson
	Far from the Madding Crowd Colin
BEN JONSON	*Volpone*
JOHN KEATS	*Selected*
RUDYARD KIPLING	*Kim* Leo
PHILIP LARKIN	*The Whits* Andrew
D.H. LAWRENCE	*Sons and Lovers* R. P. Draper

MACMILLAN MASTER GUIDES

TESS OF THE D'URBERVILLES

BY THOMAS HARDY

JAMES GIBSON

MACMILLAN

First published 1986 by
MACMILLAN PRESS LTD
Houndmills, Basingstoke, Hampshire RG21 2XS
and London
Companies and representatives
throughout the world

ISBN 0–333–37287–5

A catalogue record for this book is available
from the British Library.

11 10 9 8 7 6
03 02 01 00 99 98 97

Printed in Malaysia

CONTENTS

GENERAL EDITOR'S PREFACE

The aim of the Macmillan Master Guides is to help you to appreciate the book you are studying by providing information about it and by suggesting ways of reading and thinking about it which will lead to a fuller understanding. The section on the writer's life and background has been designed to illustrate those aspects of the writer's life which have influenced the work, and to place it in its personal and literary context. The summaries and critical commentary are of special importance in that each brief summary of the action is followed by an examination of the significant critical points. The space which might have been given to repetitive explanatory notes has been devoted to a detailed analysis of the kind of passage which might confront you in an examination. Literary criticism is concerned with both the broader aspects of the work being studied and with its detail. The ideas which meet us in reading a great work of literature, and their relevance to us today, are an essential part of our study, and our Guides look at the thought of their subject in some detail. But just as essential is the craft with which the writer has constructed his work of art, and this may be considered under several technical headings – characterisation, language, style and stagecraft, for example.

The authors of these Guides are all teachers and writers of wide experience, and they have chosen to write about books they admire and know well in the belief that they can communicate their admiration to you. But you yourself must read and know intimately the book you are studying. No one can do that for you. You should see this book as a lamppost. Use it to shed light, not to lean against. If you know your text and know what it is saying about life, and how it says it, then you will enjoy it, and there is no better way of passing an examination in literature.

JAMES GIBSON

ACKNOWLEDGEMENT

Cover illustration: Stonehenge by John Constable. © Victoria and Albert Museum, London, courtesy of the Bridgeman Art Library.

1 THOMAS HARDY: LIFE AND BACKGROUND

Thomas Hardy was born at Higher Bockhampton, close to Dorchester, a county town in the south-west of England, on 2 June 1840. Few great writers can have had as humble a birth-place as the small, secluded cottage hidden in the trees at the end of a country lane, which is now an object of pilgrimage for many thousands of his admirers each year. He lived in that cottage for the first twenty-two years of his life, growing up in the midst of a rustic environment which was to play a large part in his great novels. A boy of sensitive awareness to the life going on around him, and blest with a remarkable retentive memory, he was in those years to acquire the experience, the knowledge, the impressions which served him so well as a writer.

From his parents he inherited contrasting qualities. His mother was an earnest, characterful woman determined that he should do well in life; his father, who earned his living as a stonemason and small builder, enjoyed the life of the senses and had a passion for music which he passed on to his son. His mother bore him only six months after her marriage, and at birth he was thought to be dead until a midwife smacked him into life. He was a weakly boy, sensitive and easily moved to tears. At that time there was no universal compulsory education, but his mother sent him to the local village school when he was seven, and subsequently he became a pupil at a school in Dorchester where he stayed until he was sixteen, when his mother paid £100 – a sum of something like £3000 in modern money – for him to be apprenticed to an architect.

His architectural training in Dorchester lasted for about six years and was an influence upon him as a novelist. Whenever he describes a building, we recognise that he knows what he is talking about. But, even more important, his novels will be found to have the careful planning of an architect. The seven phases of Tess's life, into which the book is divided, provide a meticulously worked-out structure, and the novel is full of symmetries and parallels. These years from 1856–62 were years of vital and rapid development. In the *Life of Thomas Hardy by Thomas Hardy* he describes how his life at that time was 'a life twisted of three strands – the professional life, the scholar's life, and the rustic life, combined in the twenty-four hours of one day'. The architectural (i.e., professional) strand we have already mentioned. The life of a scholar is a reference to the intense programme of study he imposed on himself at that time, often rising at five in the morning in order to pursue his reading. He was as determined as his mother that he should show himself to be an educated man, and he read widely in English literature, in the Classics, and in many branches of knowledge, with a particular interest in science and philosophy. And he knew his Bible and his Shakespeare intimately; quotations from these two great books are found throughout his writing, and echoes abound.

The third strand mentioned by Hardy – the rustic life – resulted from his actually living in the heart of the country. The parish of Stinsford, in which Higher Bockhampton lay, was a community of people linked together by their past history and by their present dependence on each other. Hardy's father was a keen musician who had at one time, like his father before him, played his viol in the parish church choir. But he loved every kind of music, and when he went off to play his musical instrument at parties and weddings and feasts, he took his son, Tom, along with him. Tom himself had been taught to play the violin, and he spent many hours playing away at these functions and acquiring that knowledge of the local people, of their lives, their traditions, their stories and their songs, which enrich his writing.

It was during this period that he decided that he would like to be a writer, preferably a poet, and he began consciously to prepare himself for a profession which he greatly esteemed. To widen his horizons, and to obtain that knowledge of the world which he thought every writer should have, he left his native village in 1862 and took a job in London as a practising architect. It was a London which, with the development of the railway companies in the previous twenty years, had become very much the centre of the universe, growing and changing rapidly, and abuzz with intellectual ideas and cultural activities. New scientific discoveries had made it difficult to accept the literal truth of the Bible, the train was making people more mobile and beginning to destroy the old self-contained communities, and every idea and belief was being discussed and challenged. Hardy was very aware of all this and of the enormous changes which, beginning then, were to mark his whole life. He had loved the life of his parish church, its hymns and chants, its Bible readings and liturgy. He went on loving it for the rest of his life, but intellectually he found himself unable to accept the simple faith of his youth, and he became highly critical of the Victorian Church with its narrow morality and its uncharitable dogmatism. It is no accident that Hardy makes Parson Tringham responsible for starting the chain of events which is to lead Tess to the gallows.

Unable to get any of his poetry published, he decided to try his hand as a novelist and his first book, *Desperate Remedies*, was published in 1871. It failed, but *Under the Greenwood Tree* was more of a success when it was published in 1872, and the success of *Far from the Madding Crowd* in 1874 meant that he was able to give up architecture and become a full-time writer. In the same year he married Emma Lavinia Gifford whom he had met in Cornwall in 1870 while he was drawing up plans for the restoration of a dilapidated old church. The marriage lasted until the death of Emma in 1912, but, although it began happily, the happiness was not to last. True to Victorian convention they went on living together but there is much evidence of a lack of sympathy between them, of a wife who could not keep up with a husband who was rising in the world, and of a husband who, sensitive as he was as a writer, was insensitive to his wife's needs. It is not just chance that there are so many unhappy marriages in Hardy's later novels.

He published fourteen novels between 1871 and 1895, and through such masterpieces as *Far from the Madding Crowd*, *The Return of the Native* (1878) and *The Mayor of Casterbridge* (1885), he gradually made a name for himself among discriminating readers. But fame came only with the publication of *Tess* in 1891 and *Jude the Obscure* in 1895, and it was ironic that the enormous success of these two novels was partly due to the sensation they caused because they were attacked by so many pillars of the Establishment as unclean and unfit to be read. One noble bishop even informed the newspapers that he had burned his copy of *Jude*. Hardy, delighted as he must have been with the enormous sales which resulted from this publicity, was deeply hurt by the virulent attacks on him and decided to give up novel writing for his first love, poetry.

In 1898 he published the first of what were to be eight books of verse written between then and his death in 1928. At first he was not taken seriously as a poet, but with the publication of *The Dynasts* in 1904-8 it was gradually realised that he was not only a very great novelist, but also a very great poet. Max Gate, the solid Victorian house he had had built for himself near Dorchester in 1884-5, became a place of pilgrimage for his countless admirers, and honours were conferred on him by the State and by the universities. The boy born in such humble circumstances had become the grand old man of English letters, but he still retained much of the simple Wessex countryman he had always been, loving nothing more than to wander with his dog along the lanes and through the fields which he had immortalised in his novels. The churchyard at Stinsford, in which Emma and his ancestors were buried beneath the greenwood tree, remained a sacred place to him and he requested that he should be buried there. His request was not heeded. At his death on 11 January 1928 the Establishment demanded that he should be buried in Poets' Corner in Westminster Abbey, and after an unseemly dispute a typical but barbaric British compromise was reached. His heart was cut from his body and buried at Stinsford, the rest of him cremated and buried with the utmost ceremony in the Abbey.

2 THE WRITING, PUBLICATION AND INITIAL CRITICAL RECEPTION OF *TESS*

All but the first two of Hardy's fourteen published novels appeared first as serials in magazines and journals. The immense increase in the reading population which took place in the middle of the nineteenth century had led to a proliferation of new magazines whose readers were as hungry for serials as today's television viewers are hungry for 'soap operas'. Hardy was able to add substantially to his income through this serial publication, and when, in 1888, he first conceived the story which was eventually to become *Tess*, his intention was to sell the story, which was entitled 'Too Late Beloved', to a newspaper syndicate. However, on seeing the early chapters, the newspaper proprietors, scared of offending their readers, cancelled the contract. Hardy then offered his novel to two well-known magazines, but its 'improper explicitness' led to its again being refused. With what he called 'cynical amusement' Hardy then bowdlerised his story, omitting the drunken goings-on in Chaseborough, the seduction scene and Tess's baby. In the serial she is tricked into having a sexual relationship with Alec by his having gone through a mock marriage with her, and her leaving him is not caused by her pregnancy but by the discovery that she is not really his wife.

In its 'purer' form the novel became acceptable and it was published in *The Graphic* magazine in weekly instalments in the second half of 1891. Even so there were difficulties. The editor of *The Graphic* objected, for example, to the physical contact between Angel and the milkmaids when he carried them across the flooded stream, and Hardy had to introduce a wheelbarrow to overcome this problem. Today it hardly seems possible that such squeamishness could exist, but it is necessary to mention these publishing details in order that today's reader should have an idea of the moral outlook of the time in which *Tess* was published.

Hardy restored most of the cuts when the novel was published in three volumes in 1891, and, predictably, there was an outburst about its 'improper explicitness'. *The Quarterly Review* thought it a 'clumsy sordid tale of boorish brutality and lust'. *The Saturday Review* described it as an "unpleasant story' written in 'a very unpleasant way', and a reviewer in *The Nation* described Tess as 'a weak and sensual woman', Alec as 'an incorrigible rogue', and saw Angel as being the 'only moral character in the novel'. What seems particularly to have upset Hardy's critics was that he should have called Tess 'a pure woman'. However, there were reviewers of greater sensitivity who spoke up in the novel's defence, and Hardy must have derived some consolation from the fact that the accusation that it was a 'dirty' book led, as always, to the novel having a tremendous success in the bookshops. Overnight he went from being considered a minor novelist to being regarded as a major one. *Tess* is now thought by many to be Hardy's supreme masterpiece, a book of great sensitivity, beauty and courage which dared to challenge the most hallowed moral concepts of the Victorians, and did much to make us aware of the cruelty imposed on women by the double standards and moral dogma of that time. But the enormous changes in the moral code which have taken place since the 1890s, changes to which Hardy contributed, have not made the book seem dated, and it is now available in many different editions. Recently one of the largest publishing houses announced that of its six best-selling novels in 1983 two were by Hardy – *Far from the Madding Crowd* and *Tess*. Nearly a hundred years after their first publication there could be no greater tribute to Hardy's genius.

3 SUMMARIES AND CRITICAL COMMENTARY

3.1 PHASE THE FIRST: THE MAIDEN

Chapter 1

Summary
On his way home from Shaston market Jack Durbeyfield, the carrier, is told by Parson Tringham, the antiquary, that he is descended from the ancient and knightly family of the d'Urbervilles. The Parson's doubts about the wisdom of imparting this information to the feckless Durbeyfield are confirmed when 'Sir John' sends to the Pure Drop Inn for a horse and carriage and some rum.

Commentary
Although there is a good deal of humour in this opening chapter the action taken by the Parson – ironically the Church's representative – precipitates the tragedy. The first paragraph sets the place and time of the story, and, as so often in a Hardy novel, we are introduced to someone travelling along a road, a symbol of man as a wayfarer, of life as a journey. The theme of heredity is introduced and Jack Durbeyfield's casual, tipsy attitude to life tells us something about his character.

Chapter 2

Summary
Blackmoor Vale is described in some detail and we are told of its historic interest, the curious legend of the killing of a beautiful white hart, and of the old May Day customs which still survive. One of these is the 'club-walking' in which the women, dressed in white and with willow wands in their hands, processed through the village, and danced on the green. They see Jack riding to the Pure Drop Inn in his carriage and embarrass Tess,

his daughter, by laughing at his obvious drunkenness. Tess's beauty is described, and the red ribbon she wears in her hair. Three young men pass by the dancing, and one, Angel Clare, joins the women in spite of the puritanical protests of his two brothers, Cuthbert and Felix. Angel, by chance, does not dance with Tess but as he leaves, when the church clock strikes, he is conscious that she is hurt by the oversight and wishes that he had asked her to dance.

Commentary

Hardy introduces us to two of his main characters, Tess and Angel, and to the irony that dominates their relationship: he did not dance with her. We are made aware of Tess's beauty, her pride, her innocence. The redness of the ribbon in her hair, and the redness of her mouth begin a chain of references to that colour of blood and danger, and the striking of the church clock prefigures the striking of the hours as Tess meets her fate in the final chapter. Some of the weakness of Angel's character is suggested by 'he was a desultory tentative student of something and everything', and the puritanical aspect of his upbringing can be sensed through the reactions of his priggish brothers.

Chapter 3

Summary

Tess dances with her comrades until dusk, but worried by her father's odd appearance, returns to her cottage to find her mother doing the washing and singing to the youngest of her seven surviving children. Tess's personal charms come from her mother, whose attitude to life is summed up by 'her instinctive plan for relieving herself of her labours lay in postponing them'. Her mother tells her of their aristocratic ancestors and that her father's health is threatened by 'fat round his heart'. He has gone to Rollivers to celebrate the news of his ancestors, and his wife goes off ostensibly to bring him back but really in order to join him in his drinking. Hardy tells us that between the mother and her more educated daughter is a gap of two hundred years, her mother is Jacobean (i.e., seventeenth-century), Tess is Victorian. It grows late and Tess, worried because her father has to take a load of beehives to Casterbridge market early next day, goes off to get her parents back from the 'ensnaring inn'.

Commentary

The introduction to Tess's home and mother and her obvious concern for her parents and brothers and sisters begin to win our sympathy for her. Hardy is filling in the background and indicating the differences between daughter and parents, differences which contribute to the tragedy. The reference to Jack Durbeyfield's heart condition makes his eventual death in Chapter 50 more acceptable as a plot device, and Hardy's own sympathy for the young children of the Durbeyfield family makes him intrude very stridently in his condemnation of William Wordsworth's belief in 'Nature's holy plan'.

Chapter 4

Summary
At Rolliver's Inn, where the local people seek 'beatitude', Mrs Durbeyfield tells her husband of her plan to send Tess 'to claim kin' with 'a great rich lady out by Trantridge' in the hope that it might lead to a fine marriage. Tess comes to get them home but it is soon clear to her that her father's state of weakness through drink will make it impossible for him to take the hives to market, and that she will have to take them herself. At two o'clock in the morning she sets out with her brother, Abraham, and is so exhausted that she falls asleep. The morning mail-cart runs into them, Prince the horse is killed, and Tess, blaming herself for the death of Prince, who is vital to the livelihood of the family, sees 'herself in the light of a murderess'.

Commentary
Each incident seems to follow almost inevitably from what preceded it, and the death of Prince results from Jack Durbeyfield's inability to go to market, which results from his overdrinking, which results from Parson Tringham's indiscretion in telling him that he is 'Sir John'. The feckless character of the parents is developed in the scene at Rolliver's, and the death of Prince is described economically and powerfully to produce the maximum of emotional effect. Prince is pierced as if by a sword and Tess is splashed with his blood, an event that prefigures her own rape by Alec and Alec's death. The comic note which has been apparent in the opening chapters and which is found even in Mrs Rolliver's glib explanations of the illicit drinking party, changes in this chapter to sadness and tragedy, and Hardy's interest in the relationship between comedy and tragedy may be seen in his comment that the comical effect of Jack Durbeyfield's drunken walking was 'like most comical effects, not quite so comic after all'. Our sympathy for Tess grows as we witness her care for her parents and her sense of responsibility for her family.

Chapter 5

Summary
Tess is unwilling to seek her rich 'relations' at Trantridge as she senses the

danger there, but is forced to do so by her awareness that the death of Prince has plunged her family into penury. She walks to Shaston and takes a van from there to Trantridge Cross. Mrs d'Urberville lives in an almost new house whose red brick colour and newness contrast with the ancient forest land stretching beyond it. Hardy tells us that these d'Urbervilles are really Stokes. Mr Simon Stoke, now dead, made a great deal of money in trade in the north of England, and decided to acquire a more aristocratic name on settling in the south. Tess meets his son, Alec, and tells him that she has come because they are of the same family, and that her branch of the family has fallen on bad times. Alec immediately makes up to Tess, feeds her with a strawberry, and when Tess tells him how she killed Prince assures her that his mother will 'find a berth for you'.

Commentary

Another of the main characters, Alec, is introduced, and is immediately recognisable as the typical villain. He emerges, smoking, from the dark triangular door of the tent, has a swarthy complexion, a black moustache and a bold, rolling eye. The way he treats Tess stamps him as a womaniser and the parting of her lips when he forces a strawberry into her mouth prefigures later events. It is the meeting of innocence and experience, of the good and the bad, and Hardy, moved by the situation his imagination has created, comments that 'In the ill-judged execution of the well-judged plan of things the call seldom produces the comer, the man to love rarely coincides with the hour for loving'.

Chapter 6

Summary

Tess comes home to find that a letter has already arrived, ostensibly from Mrs d'Urberville, offering her a job looking after the poultry farm. Tess is loath to go but, a week later, she hears that Alec has called to enquire whether she intends to accept the offer, and under pressure from her family she agrees to go.

Commentary

Alec's persistence and her family's needs make it inevitable that Tess, being the person she is, will submit to the pressures on her and take the job offered with all the dangers associated with it. Tension is created by Tess's obvious fear of Alec, and her mother's unrealistic belief that Alec will marry Tess 'and make a lady of her' adds to the irony and pathos of the situation. The pricking of her chin by Alec's rose is seen by Tess as an ill omen and her superstitious belief will be shown to be well-founded.

Chapter 7

Summary
Mrs Durbeyfield insists that Tess is dressed up in her best clothes for her departure to Trantridge, and is certain that Alec will 'never have the heart not to love her' and marry her. Her tipsy father is prepared to sell his title to Alec for an amount that rapidly falls from one thousand to twenty pounds. Mother and daughters set out for the place where Tess is to be met by the vehicle which will take her to Trantridge, and all are alarmed when it turns out to be a smart gig driven by the 'horsey young buck', Alec, who quickly drives Tess away. In bed that night Mrs Durbeyfield quietens her doubts with the reflection that 'if he don't marry her afore he will after'.

Commentary
The heroine is put in peril and Hardy cleverly develops a powerful emotional situation. Tess is prepared like a sacrifice for the fate that awaits her, her innocence emphasised by the wearing of her white frock, her vulnerability by reference to the 'amplitude' of her developing figure. Her mother's casualness and her father's drunkenness aggravate the situation, and Tess's own fears when she sees that it is Alec who has come to pick her up impart themselves to her sisters and to us, the readers.

Chapter 8

Summary
Alec shows off and tries to frighten Tess into putting her arms around him by driving the dog-cart downhill at a reckless speed. Eventually she is forced by her fear into allowing him to give her 'the kiss of mastery'. By letting her hat blow off she is able to alight from the vehicle and she then insists on walking to Trantridge, aware that much as she would like to return home her resolve to help her family will not allow her to do so.

Commentary
The shape of the threat to Tess becomes manifest. Alec's cruelty to his horse, significantly a mare, which he has whipped into submission, tells us a good deal about him, and to him Tess is a mere 'cottage girl'. He takes shameless advantage of her youth and begins his merciless sexual attack on her. But we see something of Tess's own spirit in her fighting response to him, and there are premonitions of the future in the references to killing, to the breaking of necks, and in Alec's 'kinsman be hanged'. We are forced to read on by our anxiety to know whether the villain will wreak his will

on the heroine. Hardy is handling one of the oldest clichés in fiction with extraordinary richness and subtlety.

Chapter 9

Summary
We find Tess looking after the fowls at The Slopes at Trantridge. She lives in an old, thatched cottage surrounded by a wall, and, as part of her duties, she takes the fowls each day to the adjacent mansion to be felt and fondled by Mrs d'Urberville. Tess is surprised to find that Alec's mother is old and blind.

Commentary
Tess is made even more vulnerable by the blindness of Mrs d'Urberville and Alec keeps up his attack on Tess by a mixture of flattery and pretence of caring for her.

Chapter 10

Summary
Every Saturday night, when work is finished, the young people of Trantridge make their way to Chaseborough, 'a decayed market-town', in order to drink and enjoy themselves. Tess, enjoying the outing, often goes too, sometimes independently but always returning with her companions in order to have their protection. One Saturday in September Tess, watched by Alec, goes to meet her friends and finds them in an outhouse, dancing and more than usually 'lit up'. It is very late when they set out on the three-mile walk home and Tess is attacked by one of the looser women in the party when she laughs at a mishap which occurs. Alec arrives and carries Tess off on his horse, leaving the drunken workfolk to make their way home while commenting that Tess has moved 'out of the frying-pan into the fire!'

Commentary
The Saturday night 'entertainment' at the aptly named Chaseborough provides Alec with the moment he has been waiting for. He saves Tess from a minor trouble and has the opportunity of becoming her destroyer. The two Queens, of Spades and Diamonds, have already experienced Alec's sexual attentions and they coarsely snigger at the fate which they know awaits Tess. Hardy is building up to his climax with great care. Tess's innocence and loveliness is shown in stark contrast to the drinking and loose behaviour so strikingly depicted in this chapter, which, because

of its outspoken material, had to be omitted from the serial appearance of the story.

Chapter 11

Summary
Alec gallops away with Tess into the Chase – 'the oldest wood in England'. Tess is desperately tired, the night is foggy, and Alec works on her by appearing to care for her safety and by mentioning that he has sent her father a new horse, and her brothers and sisters some toys. Then he deliberately loses his way, makes 'a sort of couch or nest' for Tess among the dead leaves and goes off to ascertain their whereabouts. He returns to find her asleep and 'the coarse appropriates the finer', Tess is deflowered.

Commentary
The climax has been reached, the maiden loses her maidenhead. This must have been a difficult chapter for Hardy to write because the seduction (rape?) of Tess had to be suggested rather than described. But it is carefully motivated and immensely poignant. Tess is worn down by Alec's constant siege, her sense that she ought to be grateful to him, her physical exhaustion. What chance has innocence, Hardy seems to be saying, against such a combination of fate and cunning experience? Hardy's pity for Alec's victim suffuses these pages and forces him to ask why, why, why? And we, too, our sympathy for Tess won by Hardy's vivid imaginative creation of her, repeat after him 'There lay the pity of it'.

3.2 PHASE THE SECOND: MAIDEN NO MORE

Chapter 12

Summary
It is about four months after Tess's arrival at Trantridge and a 'few weeks subsequent to the night ride in the Chase'. Tess, heavily laden, is walking home on a Sunday morning when Alec comes chasing after her in his gig. He asks her why she has slipped away from The Slopes so stealthily. She refuses to return and in tears tells him that 'if I had ever sincerely loved you, if I loved you still, I should not so loathe and hate myself for my weakness as I do now'. Finding that she won't return he tells her to get in touch with him 'if certain circumstances should arise', and rides off. She meets a man whose fervour drives him to paint religious texts on walls, gates and stiles, and she is horrified by the relevance to herself of the particular text which he is at that moment painting in red letters

on a stile. On arriving home her mother soon realises that she is pregnant and criticises her for not getting Alec to marry her. Tess passionately accuses her mother of having failed to warn her of the dangers she had been exposed to, and Mrs Durbeyfield replies, 'Tis nater, after all, and what do please God!'

Commentary
The word 'maiden' had strong connotations of virginity in Wessex in Victorian times, hence the significance of 'Maiden No More'. It is now late October. Hardy has discreetly passed over the period of time since the incident in the Chase, but subtle suggestions of the relationship between Tess and Alec may be found in the fact that Alec knows that she has slipped away from her bed early on a Sunday morning and in Tess's, 'if I had ever sincerely loved you . . . ' and 'My eyes were dazed by you for a little . . . '. Just as there are hints that Tess has had a sexual relationship with Alec subsequent to the seduction, so the reader is given hints of the reason for her leaving The Slopes. Alec's, 'if certain circumstances should arise' and Tess's, 'If I did love you, I may have the best o' causes for letting you know it. But I don't' prefigure the birth of Sorrow, and 'in the cause of her confidence her sorrow lay' may be a further reference to the situation which Hardy purposely leaves indistinct. Tess's impetuous rage at Alec's chauvinistic generalisations about women shows an important aspect of her character, while her comment, 'See how you've mastered me' is another significant comment on Alec's domination of her. The incident with the painter of religious graffiti gives Hardy the opportunity of exposing the Church's rigid and merciless code, while the return home enables him to show the contrast between Mrs Durbeyfield's insensitive but natural down-to-earth opportunism and Tess's honest refusal to ask for favours from a man she despises.

Chapter 13

Summary
The reaction of the local girls to Tess's 'state' is described, and Hardy cleverly examines the reaction of Tess's mother, and of Tess herself. The local girls even feel some kind of envy for her, but Tess's momentary elation at this is soon destroyed by 'cold reason' when she thinks of the 'long and stony highway which she had to tread, without aid, and with little sympathy'. The power of music over Tess, when she goes to church, is described, as are her solitary evening walks through a countryside which is more in harmony with her than she thinks.

Commentary

A chapter of little action. The baby has not yet been born, and Hardy looks at the contrast between Tess's deep sense of guilt and betrayal and the far more natural reaction of her girl friends who, in some ways, even envy her. He emphasises too, that it is she who is in harmony with the natural world, and that if only she had not been obsessed by 'shreds of convention' and 'a cloud of moral hobgoblins', she need not have regarded herself as being 'such an anomaly'. Hardy's passionate condemnation of the unnaturalness of the moral convention of the time makes this an important narratorial statement.

Chapter 14

Summary

It is August, some ten months since Tess returned to her home from The Slopes. The four red arms of a reaping machine are described as they cut the corn while the men and women bind the sheaves. Tess is among the women and as the day wears on her 'feminine smoothness becomes scari- fied by the stubble, and bleeds'. When the workers break for lunch Tess's sister brings her the baby to feed, and the workfolk comment upon her love for the child and on how it was begot. Tess works on until the evening and arrives home to find that her baby has been taken ill and seems likely to die. She is horrified at the thought of his dying unbaptised, and when her father, because of his sense of the 'smudge' Tess has brought upon the family, refuses to allow the parson to enter his house to carry out the baptism, Tess baptises the child herself. The baby dies and, refused a Christian burial by the parson, is buried 'in that shabby corner of God's allotment . . . where all unbaptized infants, notorious drunkards, suicides, and others of the conjecturally damned are laid'.

Commentary

Hardy's love for his creation, Tess, and his passionate concern for her are nowhere felt more strongly than in this richly textured chapter. It begins with the reaping of the corn in all the beauty of an autumn landscape, and ends with the reaping of Tess's aptly named illegitimate child, Sorrow. Tess becomes the symbolic field-woman and is identified with her natural surroundings. But all is not idyllic. The scarlet reaping machine is a sign of the progress which is to destroy the old farming ways, and the animals caught in the centre of the field by the reaping are 'every one put to death by the sticks and stones of the harvesters'. The work is hard and Tess's arm bleeds from the scarifying of the stubble, and we are moved by her strangely mixed feelings about her child. Her love for the baby and the desire that he should not be consigned to Hell because he has not been baptised win our sympathy for her, and we share Hardy's contempt for a Church which has allowed its charity to be less important than its dogmatic tenets. The cross of two lathes and the marmalade jar provide that kind of realistic detail which Hardy uses so well, and they add to the pathos of a scene which increases our sympathy for the suffering woman.

Chapter 15

Summary
Hardy comments on how often we learn from experience too late for the lesson to be of value to us, as has happened with Tess. Time slips away and Tess changes from 'simple girl to complex woman'. In spite of her sad experiences, 'the pulse of hopeful life' is warm within her and, knowing that she could not be comfortable in her home village, Marlott, she takes a post as a milkmaid at a dairy called Talbothays many miles to the south, and, at the thought of the new life opening to her the spirit within her 'rose automatically as the sap in the twigs'.

Commentary
Little happens in this chapter, but time passes, Tess recovers, and Hardy prepares us for the next phase in her life. Again he emphasises that what has happened to Tess would have been no more than a 'liberal education' if it had not been for the 'world's opinion'. For him Tess is guiltless, and his belief in life, which gives the lie to those who regard Hardy as a pessimist, can be seen in his description of the recuperative power which pervades organic nature, and which brings with it 'hope, and the invincible instinct towards self-delight'.

3.3 PHASE THE THIRD: THE RALLY

Chapter 16

Summary
It is May, two and a half years after Tess's return home from her sojourn at The Slopes, and she is again on the road travelling. She passes through Stourcastle and Weatherbury, and finally comes to Talbothays farm in the Valley of the Great Dairies. Tess's spirits rise as she surveys 'the valley in which milk and butter grew to rankness' and feels the 'clear, bracing ethereal air', and she bursts out in a psalm of praise to the Lord. She arrives at the farm as the dairymen are calling in the cows for milking.

Commentary

A chapter of great beauty in which Tess's reawakening to life seems to become part of the great awakening of nature in the spring. Hardy emphasises that she sets out in a direction almost opposite to that of her first journey to The Slopes. He is fond of that kind of directional symbolism, and contrast is brought in by the reference to the intrinsic difference between the Vale of the Little Dairies and this new, life-enhancing Valley of the Great Dairies. In her new surroundings Tess hears a 'pleasant voice in every breeze', and Hardy's affirmation of the primacy of the life-giving forces is heard in 'The irresistible, universal, automatic tendency to find sweet pleasure somewhere, which pervades all life, from the meanest to the highest had at last mastered Tess'; this mastering is of a different quality from the mastering by Alec. There is life, there is hope, but an augury of the future may be seen in the description of Tess as 'like a fly on a billiard table'. Life for all its beauty still has an impersonal cruelty and we are reminded of Shakespeare's 'Like flies to wanton boys are we to the gods'. But then, changing his perspective, Hardy gives us the carefully observed detail of the 'red and white herd', the 'long thatched sheds' with 'their slopes encrusted with vivid green moss', to be followed by the wooden 'posts rubbed to a glossy smoothness by the flanks of infinite cows and calves of bygone years', and then again, that distancing, that reminder of time passing which he does so superbly, for those infinite cows and calves have 'passed to an oblivion almost inconceivable in its profundity'.

Chapter 17

Summary

The milking of the cows begins, and we are introduced to Mr Crick, the master-dairyman, who greets Tess warmly. She is keen to begin work right away and joins the milkers. They sing songs to help with their work and Dairyman Crick tells a tale about a bull which is 'softened down' by having a fiddle played to him. As the conversation goes on, Tess becomes aware of a man milking who differs from the rest by virtue of being 'educated, reserved, subtle, sad'. She recognises him as the pedestrian who had joined in the club-dance at Marlott but not danced with her. She sleeps with three other milkmaids in a large room over the milk-house, and she learns from them that the strange young man is Mr Angel Clare who plays the harp and is 'learning farming in all its branches'. His father is a vicar at Emminster. She falls asleep to 'the measured dripping of the whey from the wrings downstairs'.

Commentary

In a poem called 'Afterwards' which Hardy wrote about his own death he describes himself as a 'man who used to notice such things'. His knowledge of dairy farming plays an important part in these early chapters of 'The Rally'. The dairy scene is described in such a way that we feel its authenticity. In the first paragraph of this chapter the observation that the girls milk with their faces sideways, their right cheeks resting against the cows, while the male milkers gaze at the ground is the kind of detail that makes the reader feel in the hands of an expert, and a great deal can be learnt about dairy farming at that time from Hardy's perceptive comments. All this adds great richness to the scene. As part of the temporary lightening of the atmosphere which is a vital part of the structure of the story, humour is introduced in the anecdote about William Dewy playing his fiddle to the bull. The time has come for Angel to be brought back into the story, and Hardy begins to establish his character and provide information about him and his background. There is a delicate irony in the fact that he is not only called Angel but also plays a harp.

Chapter 18

Summary

We are told just how Angel comes to be at the farm. His father, an earnest Low Church clergyman, had assumed that Angel would follow his older brothers into the ministry, but Angel is critical of Church dogma and finds himself unable to become an ordained clergyman. As a result he is denied an education at Cambridge, spends some years in desultory studies, is nearly 'entrapped by a woman much older than himself', and eventually decides to become a farmer. At the age of twenty-six he has come to Talbothays as a student and lives in an immense attic above the dairy-house. But he learns not only about cows but about humans. He becomes acquainted with 'the seasons in their moods' and he begins to realise that the country-folk are all unique individuals. As the chapter ends he becomes aware of Tess, of her 'fluty voice' and her belief that 'souls can be made to go outside our bodies', and he decides that he must have seen her somewhere in the past.

Commentary

The narrative requires Angel to become aware of Tess, and interested in her, and this is now achieved. We need to know about his religious background because this will help to explain his later treatment of her. It also enables Hardy to state his own case against 'an untenable redemptive theolatry'. The character of Mr Clare – 'straightforward and simple-minded' – is also developed as he will play an important minor part in the story.

Hardy very much resents the tendency of many people to see all agricultural workers as 'typical and unvarying' Hodges and he makes the point
through Angel's awakening awareness of the uniqueness of every one of
his companions on the farm. There is a prefiguring of coming events in
the description of the dairyman's knife and fork as being 'like the begin-
nings of a gallows', and in Angel's opening description of Tess as being
like a 'fresh and virginal daughter of Nature' there is a hint of the trouble
to come.

Chapter 19

Summary
The chapter opens with another description of the milking and of Angel's
efforts to see that Tess gets the cows that she likes. On 'a typical summer
evening in July' she is deeply moved by hearing Angel play his harp.
When he talks to her he is puzzled that so young a girl should be so full of
'sad imaginings'. He asks her why but she cannot tell him of the tragic
event in her life, nor can she understand why he, a man of good family
and education, should also be so melancholy about life. They continue
to talk together as the days pass and Tess wonders whether Angel might
be impressed by learning of her aristocratic ancestors, but is told by the
dairyman that Angel despises old families, and Tess decides to keep quiet.

Commentary
We learn about the milking and witness the gradual growing together of
Angel and Tess. Her listening to his playing of the harp as she stands
among the 'tall blooming weeds' is described with a rich sensuousness,
and again the reader is brought close to Tess as she is rendered unconscious
of time and space by the effect his playing has on her. But always within
the beautiful setting there are undertones of sadness, forebodings of the
future, as if the devil lurked in the undergrowth of what should be a paradise. The reference to Tess's Sixth Standard training is important because
it is to some extent that partial education which is responsible for her
sense of guilt, not shared by her uneducated mother, and for her experience of the 'ache of modernism', that fear of life which has come with
the loss of faith in a divine order controlling all our doings. Tess's state
is brilliantly illustrated by the contrast between her simple folkish picking
and peeling of the buds called 'lords and ladies' and the philosophic discussion she enters into with Angel. This conflict within Tess herself is a
vital part of the story. Tess's meditating on life permits Hardy to put over
what are almost certainly some of his own views and to ask questions which
thinking humans have repeatedly asked. Why does the sun 'shine on the
just and the unjust alike?' There is a growing self-identification of the writer

with his heroine, she becomes ever more the means of expressing feelings and ideas which are central to him and his story, his involvement with Tess and love of his own creation are increasingly manifest in this phase of the book. As the chapter closes there is irony in the dairyman's disclosure that Angel despises the old aristocratic families, but it should be noticed that Hardy describes this as a 'caricature of Clare's opinions'.

Chapter 20

Summary
The summer develops and Angel and Tess converge 'under an irresistible law, as surely as two streams in one vale'. This is possibly Tess's happiest time and to Angel she becomes a 'visionary essence of woman'. As they milk together in the early morning Tess sometimes looks like a divinity, sometimes a dazzlingly fair dairymaid.

Commentary
The miracle of rebirth in springtime and life's ephemeral nature are powerfully described, and Hardy emphasises that Tess and Angel are as much under the irresistible law of nature as are the flowers and the birds. Angel's growing love for Tess is seen in their working relationship. Rising a little after 3am to milk the cows, he and she are compared to Adam and Eve, and Tess's symbolic nature is brought out in Angel's seeing her as 'a visionary essence of woman'. But already we see in his wish to think of her as Artemis, the Greek goddess of chastity, the dangerous tendency to idealise her and love the idea rather than the woman. There is significance in her request to him to 'Call me Tess'. The final description of the milking in the foggy mornings is a great passage of poetic prose, rich with repeated sounds, fine images, and highly imaginative and densely packed details.

Chapter 21

Summary
There is consternation in the milk-house when the milk refuses to be churned into butter. It is suggested that this is because somebody is in love, and dairyman Crick tells a seemingly funny story of a character called Jack Dollop who scrambles into a churn to escape from the mother of a girl he has wronged, is found in that situation and churned by the mother until he agrees to marry her daughter. Tess, who sees in the story an echo of her own, is distressed. As she dozes in bed that night she hears the other three milkmaids – Retty Priddle, Izz Huett and Marian – looking

out at Angel in the garden and expressing their love for him, but Marian points out that he loves Tess best. Tess is saddened by the situation and worried by the belief that after what happened with Alec she 'could never allow any man to marry her now'.

Commentary

The clouds begin to gather. Hardy exploits very cleverly the amusing story of Jack Dollop, but comedy and tragedy are closely allied and Tess is sadly moved by recollections of her own betrayal. That ability she has of thinking too precisely on the event is manifest again at the end of the chapter where her sense of guilt makes her think that she could never conscientiously marry Angel. The last paragraph describes the situation as Tess sees it. Hardy has already made it clear that he does not share her feeling that her past experiences have sullied her and made her unfit to be another man's wife. Note the subtle touch of the dairyman calling her 'maidy', with its connotations of virginity (as in his description of Jack Dollop's 'poor maid – or young woman, rather'), and Hardy's growing equation of Angel with the sun. Tess feels that she ought not to sun herself in Angel's eyes.

Chapter 22

Summary

There is more consternation when a customer complains about a twang in the butter, and all the dairy-folk set out to find the shoots of garlic which have caused the trouble. As they stand together in the fields Tess tries to draw Angel's attention to the attractions of the other dairymaids, and she attempts in the succeeding days to avoid him and to give the other three girls every chance.

Commentary

The description of the search for the garlic plants provides another fascinating picture of life on a dairy farm at that time, and Hardy uses it once again to show the individuality of the workers. It is typical of his realism that even in the lovely settings of Talbothays in the summer, we are told that 'flaxen Frances' is 'consumptive from the winter damps of the water-meads'. The reader's sympathy for Tess is increased by her self-sacrificing attempt to sing the praises of the other milkmaids to Angel, and in the final paragraph of the chapter there is an implicit contrast between what Tess sees as Angel's care not to compromise the happiness of the dairymaids by taking sexual advantage of their passion for him and what would have been Alec's behaviour in similar circumstances. But there may be just a suggestion by Hardy in the words 'what she deemed . . . the self-controlling

22

sense of duty shown by him' that Angel also lacks Alec's strong sexual
drive, something which will become important on Tess's wedding night.
The last few words in the chapter – from 'and in the absence of' to the end
– are not found in the serial.

Chapter 23

Summary
It is now July, and on a Sunday morning the four milkmaids set out for
Mellstock church. They find the lane partly under water, and Angel,
who has spotted them in their predicament, carries them one by one
across the fifty yards of flooded lane. He whispers to Tess as she is in
his arms that he has done it all for the pleasure of carrying her, but he
draws back from declaring his love. The other milkmaids realise that
Tess is preferred by him but they bear her no malice. That night in the
dairymaids' bedroom the air seems to 'palpitate with the hopeless passion
of the girls', and, unable to sleep, they mention to Tess that Angel's
family have chosen for him 'a young lady of his own rank to marry'. Tess
is left feeling that Angel's attentions to her must mean nothing and that,
anyway, she was the least worthy of him.

Commentary
The incident of the flooded lane, on what Hardy significantly calls 'this
Suns-day, when flesh went forth to coquet with flesh while hypocritically
affecting business with spiritual things', marks another significant step
in the love relationship. Angel holds Tess in his arms and wants to kiss her.
Note how Hardy differentiates the other three dairymaids so that they
each have an individuality of their own: 'Marian had been like a sack of
meal . . . Izz had ridden sensibly and calmly. Retty was a bunch of hysterics'.
Tess, significantly, is 'like an undulating billow warmed by the sun'.
There is another implied contrast with Alec when we are told that Angel
is worried about unfairly taking advantage of Tess while she is in his arms.
The other dairymaids, accepting that Tess is Angel's favourite, are described
as 'generous young souls; they had been reared in the lonely country
nooks where fatalism is a strong sentiment, and they did not blame her'.
Tess's difference from them is well brought out here because she lacks
their fatalism and does blame herself. And Hardy seems to be excusing
them all when he describes them as writhing 'feverishly under the oppressiveness of an emotion thrust on them by cruel Nature's law'. The reference
to the 'young lady of his own rank' prepares us for the arrival in the story
of Mercy Chant.

Chapter 24

Summary
July passes into August. It is hot and 'the landscape seemed lying in a swoon'. The cows are now milked in the meadows because it is cooler. As Angel milks his cow he is overcome with love for Tess, and, moving quickly towards her, clasps her in his arms. Tess, overcome, cries, and Angel declares his love for her, and 'something had occurred which changed the pivot of the universe for their two natures'.

Commentary
Hardy concludes this phase of Tess's life with what should have been the right and proper conclusion to all those months of falling in love in the lush fields of the river Frome. Angel takes Tess into his arms and declares his love for her, but, not knowing the secret which so worries her, he can have no idea of the consternation she feels and of the struggle within her. It is part of the story's strength that we, the readers, know more than Angel does, and, at a first reading, we read on, anxious to know whether Tess's secret will be revealed. A hint about Angel's character is conveyed in the observation that he lets out a 'curious sigh of desperation, signifying unconsciously that his heart had outrun his judgment'. There is yet another evocative and detailed description, this time of the overpowering heat of summer, in the opening paragraphs. It is entirely appropriate that 'Amid the oozing fatness and warm ferments . . . when the rush of juices could almost be heard below the hiss of fertilization' Angel should find himself overcome by his passion for Tess whose red lip is so 'distracting, infatuating, maddening'. It is worth considering carefully Hardy's shrewd observation that 'it was the touch of the imperfect upon the would-be perfect that gave the sweetness, because it was that which gave the humanity'. Again there is an implied contrast between Angel's approach to love-making and Alec's.

3.4 PHASE THE FOURTH: THE CONSEQUENCE

Chapter 25

Summary
Angel is perplexed by what has happened to him and how his falling in love has changed his attitude to the farm, but his conscience worries him and he 'decides to hold aloof for the present from occupations in which they would be mutually engaged', while he considers his position. Then, one morning Dairyman Crick announces that Angel has gone home to

Emminster for a few days, and the milkmaids are stricken with gloom. The action switches to Emminster where on his way home he sees Mercy Chant, whom his parents hope that he will marry one day. His father, mother and two brothers – the Reverend Felix and the Reverend Cuthbert – are eating their morning meal, and Hardy describes the father and his religious faith in some detail. Angel is conscious of the gap between the 'transcendental aspirations' of the Emminster vicarage and the 'great passionate pulse of existence' he has known at Talbothays. He finds himself critical of the limited views of his brothers and upset at the fact that Mrs Crick's gifts to the family of black puddings had been given away to the parishioners.

Commentary
Hardy's description of Angel's confused state and of the difference falling in love has made to him is psychologically convincing, and Angel's decision to go home to see whether this will help him to sort things out is natural in the circumstances. This gives Hardy the opportunity of contrasting the narrow Hebraic life of the Emminster vicarage with the 'aesthetic, sensuous pagan pleasure in natural life' which Angel has been experiencing on the dairy-farm. There is also an implied contrast between the 'highly starched' Mercy Chant and Tess. Hardy portrays Angel's two brothers as insufferably snobbish, prudish prigs, but Angel's father has a kind heart, a sincerity, and a passion for converting sinners that will be important later on in the story. The final incident in which the vicar and his wife give away the black puddings so kindly given to them by Mrs Crick is cleverly conceived to show how kindness to one person may, paradoxically, be unkindness to another. Angel is again associated with the sun when we are told that with his departure the milkmaids felt as if 'the sunshine of the morning went out at a stroke'.

Chapter 26

Summary
Angel discusses marriage with his parents, who are keen for him to marry Mercy Chant, and Angel tells them of Tess's virtues. She possesses 'every qualification to be the helpmate of an agriculturalist', is 'chaste as a vestal' and 'a lady . . . in feeling and nature'. His parents advise him not to act in a hurry and will not object to seeing her. His father accompanies him a little way along the road back to Talbothays and tells him of his attempt to convert an evil-living young man called d'Urberville and how he had been insulted for his pains. However, he remains hopeful that 'those poor words of mine may spring up in his heart as a good seed some day'.

Commentary

The characters of Mr and Mrs Clare are developed in a chapter which acts as a marked contrast to the surrounding chapters about life at Talbothays. Angel's father is shown to be narrow and rigid in his religious views but to possess a courage, kindness, an unworldliness and humanity which are lacking in the two brothers, who represent all that is worst in institutionalised religion. The contrast between the woman the parents would like Angel to marry and the woman he wants to marry, and his singing of Tess's praises, enable Hardy to make some shrewd points about the two different ways of life, and upon what is required for domestic happiness. Angel's insistence upon her simple faith and her chastity are important, and his talk to his parents causes him to examine his own reasons for loving Tess. The introduction of Alec, 'the young upstart squire', as one Mr Clare has failed to convert reminds us that he is still there, a dark shadow in the background of the story.

Chapter 27

Summary

Angel returns to the dairy in the heat of the afternoon as the 'denizens were all enjoying the usual afternoon nap', and meets Tess coming down the stairs, her face 'flushed with sleep'. Overcome by her beauty, he asks Tess to marry him, and she, as an honourable woman, feels it necessary to refuse him. He cannot understand why, if she loves him, she does so, but hopes that with time she may change her mind. He rejects her half-hearted excuse that his parents would not approve of the marriage by telling her that they are simple-mannered, unambitious people. Then he tells Tess of his father's encounter with Alec d'Urberville, which fortifies Tess's belief that she cannot possibly marry him.

Commentary

The love affair is taken a stage further by Angel's offer of marriage, and Hardy skilfully develops the tension felt within Tess by the clash between what she passionately desires and what her conscience tells her she must do. The difference between life at the vicarage and life on the dairy-farm is strongly conveyed by Angel's feeling that as he returns to Talbothays it is like 'throwing off splints and bandages'. There is a strongly physical and erotic description of Tess, the red interior of her mouth, her naked arm and her neck, and looking as 'warm as a sunned cat'. The intense physicality of Tess is conveyed by such means and we are able to experience Angel's awareness of her. Hardy again uses the Garden of Eden imagery when Tess is described as regarding Angel 'as Eve at her second waking might have regarded Adam'. Tess's reference to the sorrow she feels at not being able to concentrate in church brings in an echo of the sad burial of her baby, Sorrow, and perhaps suggests a subconscious antipathy, just as the reference by Angel to the 'lax young cynic' brings Alec back into the story like a fate which cannot be escaped. The description of the dairy in the second paragraph of the chapter is a particularly fine piece of description, making effective use of visual and aural detail and striking imagery in order to establish our return with Angel to the world of Talbothays.

Chapter 28

Summary

It is now September and Angel keeps up the pressure on Tess to be his wife, while Tess struggles 'by every means in her power' to fortify her resolution that she cannot marry him. Desperately, she agrees that on Sunday she will give her reasons for being unable to marry, but 'In reality, she was drifting into acquiescence'. As the weekend approaches she is in an agony of indecision.

Commentary

Hardy lets us experience Tess's emotions as the struggle between her love and her sense of guilt rends her. This anguish keeps the reader in suspense and builds up our sympathy for the suffering which is blighting what should be an idyllic romance. There is more passionate writing in the incident at cheese-making when Angel kisses the inside vein of Tess's soft arm and the blood is 'driven to her finger-ends'. Angel's persistence in wooing her in spite of her protestations is important in view of his later behaviour, while her gradual acquiescence is seen by Hardy as the triumph of nature 'in revolt against her scrupulousness'. The reference to the sun (Angel?), the moon (chastity) and the willows (symbols of unhappy love), at the end of the chapter seem to presage coming events, and when we re-read the story we recognise a constant prefiguring of coming events in such remarks as Angel's, 'But you will make me happy!' and Tess's reply, 'Ah – you think so, but you don't know!'

Chapter 29

Summary

Farmer Crick at breakfast tells his workfolk of the further adventures of Jack Dollop and these relate so closely to Tess's own position, and the question of whether a woman ought to tell of any impediments before marriage, that she is greatly distressed. In the meadows Angel continues his wooing of her and Tess, increasingly convinced that his is a love that can endure all, finds herself weakening in her resolve. At the end of the chapter Angel volunteers to take the milk to the station and he asks Tess to accompany him.

Commentary

Hardy is fascinated by the concept that what may be comedy to some may be tragedy to others, and he again exploits the amusing adventures of Jack Dollop by using Dairyman Crick's story to point up Tess's predicament – to tell or not to tell. There is humour in the conversation with its culmination in Beck Knibbs's, 'All's fair in love and war'. There is great irony in Tess's growing belief that, so ardent is his wooing, he will 'love and cherish and defend her under any conditions, changes, charges, or revelations'. Hardy's sensitive awareness of women is seen when in response to Angel's glib assumption that 'Our tremulous lives are so different from theirs', she replies, 'There are very few women's lives that are not – tremulous'. The description of Tess's 'hanging tail of hair' again sounds an ominous and prefiguring note of her final fate.

Chapter 30

Summary

Angel and Tess drive with the milk to the station. In the dusk it begins to rain and Angel invites Tess to creep closer to him. On their way they pass Egdon Heath and Angel points out the remains of a manor, once one of the seats of the d'Urbervilles. The milk is loaded on to the train and on the return journey Angel again brings up the question of marriage. Tess tries to tell him about her relationship with Alec, but her courage fails her and she makes it sound as if her secret is no more than that she is descended from the d'Urbervilles. Angel tells her that, though he hates 'the aristocratic principle of blood', because of his affection for her he will 'rejoice in her descent', and it may even make his mother think better of her. Finally, Tess agrees to marry him, he kisses her and she kisses him passionately, overcome by the 'appetite for joy' which pervades all creation. Tess says that she must write to her mother in Marlott and Angel realises that he has met Tess before.

Commentary

An important chapter, because at last Tess agrees to marry Angel in spite of her inability to tell him of her past. At one moment she is so close to doing so, but Angel makes it difficult by his whimsical treatment of her. There is an obvious contrast between her journey with Alec in his gig when he gives her 'the kiss of mastery' and this journey with Angel in the spring-cart when Angel learns 'what an impassioned woman's kisses were

like upon the lips of one whom she loved with all her heart and soul'.
Hardy shows courage in making this kind of statement about women's
ability to love, and he again holds forth about the tremendous power of
love and the 'appetite for joy' which mean so much to him. Accusations
that Hardy is a pessimist are hardly borne out by such statements, even if
realistically he knows that man's weaknesses threaten that joy. Angel's
equivocation about Tess's ancestral background perhaps tells us something
of his character, of his own uncertainties and inconsistencies.

Chapter 31

Summary
Tess writes to her mother for advice and in her reply Joan Durbeyfield
tells her that on no account should she 'say a word about your Bygone
Trouble to him'. It is now October and Tess's love for Angel and worship
of him is described, together with their walks through the autumn fields.
But though she walks 'in brightness', Tess is aware of 'shapes of darkness'
threatening her. One evening, in the farmhouse by themselves, he asks her
to name the day of their wedding, but Tess is not keen to do so. When the
dairy folk return Angel tells them that he is to marry Tess, and the other
dairymaids are distressed even though they generously acknowledge Tess's
superior claims to Angel. Tess is so moved by their generosity of spirit
that she decides that she must somehow tell her history to Angel 'rather
than preserve a silence which might be deemed a treachery to him, and
which somehow seemed a wrong to these'.

Commentary
As in so many of the chapters in this Phase the irony is laid on heavily
as Tess sees Angel almost as some kind of god – 'disinterested, chivalrous,
protective' – and he talks about the distinction of being numbered 'among
those who are true, and honest, and just, and pure, and lovely, and of good
report'. His contempt for conventions is particularly ironic in the light of
his treatment of Tess on their wedding night. The imagery in this chapter
is interesting. Tess had been caught 'like a bird in a springe' (trap), while
her tread is 'like the skim of a bird'; and Hardy's sympathy for birds
is seen later in the incident of the wounded pheasants. Angel's belief that
Tess's relationship with the ancient d'Urberville family 'is a grand card to
play' not only reminds us of her mother's remark at the end of Chapter 7
that Tess's face is her 'trump card', but it also casts doubt again on his own
dogmatic statements about the aristocracy. Her mother's realistic, if dis-
honest, advice to keep quiet, which comes at the beginning of the chapter
neatly balances Tess's honest decision at the end of the chapter to confess
all to Angel. The tension is powerfully maintained by Tess's vacillation,

and the reader feels the pity of it that a love affair which has such idyllic and romantic overtones has this constant threat to it: the shapes of darkness are constantly in the background. Our respect for Tess is built up by Dairyman Crick's tribute to her, she is a 'prize for any man', and there is the further irony that it is Tess's honesty which represents the greatest danger to her.

Chapter 32

Summary
November arrives and Tess still hasn't agreed to the date of the wedding. The reduction in the milking leads to the dairyman suggesting that Tess's employment should end when Angel leaves at Christmas and that he should take her with him. Tess then fixes the date, 31 December, and fatalistically accepts the situation. Angel wishes to study the working of a flour-mill and plans to do so at Wellbridge, where, attracted by the possibility of having lodgings at a mansion which had once been in the possession of the d'Urberville family, he decides that they shall spend their honeymoon. He arranges for the wedding by licence and buys clothing for her including her wedding costume.

Commentary
The change from summer to autumn to the beginning of winter is an important background to a story in which there are increasing signs of the trouble to come. If only, as Tess says, 'it would always be summer and autumn'. Tess still cannot accept the situation entirely fatalistically, she is still full of worries, and Angel's choice of Wellbridge Manor, with its association with the d'Urbervilles, for their honeymoon is ominous. We should note, too, Hardy's description of Tess's 'passive responsiveness' which tells us a great deal about one aspect of her character. But how can she doubt her Angel when he tells her, 'I don't like you to be left anywhere away from my protection and sympathy', and how hollow and ironic these words will soon become!

Chapter 33

Summary
Angel and Tess go shopping in the local town where a man describes her as a 'comely maid', while his partner, whom Tess seems to recognise as a man from Trantridge, says that she is no maid. Angel overhears and strikes the man who has been rude to her; he apologises but later tells his companion that it was not a mistake. Angel has a dream in which he

imagines he is fighting the man who had been rude to Tess, and she, alarmed, decides to tell him of her past by writing a letter to him confessing all. She slips the note under his door. Next day Angel behaves as if nothing has happened and remains 'frank and affectionate'. The wedding day, New Year's Eve, arrives, and Tess discovers that her letter of confession had gone under the carpet of Angel's room and not been read by him. She decides that it is now too late for him to read it, and destroys it. She again tries to tell him orally of her past, but he brushes her wish to confess aside. The marriage takes place and Tess takes her vows in an 'ecstatic solemnity'. But the bad omens continue. She imagines that she has seen before the old coach which takes them to and from the church. Angel tells her of the well-known superstition that a dreadful crime had been committed once by a d'Urberville in the family coach, and she wonders whether to see or hear it is a sign of death to come or of a crime committed. They leave for their honeymoon and there is another bad omen as a cock crows three times, a sound which when heard in the afternoon is a premonition of evil.

Commentary

The climax of this phase of Tess's life approaches. In spite of every attempt by Tess to confess she still goes to the altar with Angel believing her to be a virgin and obsessed with his idea of purity. The ultimate irony is that her letter should have failed to reach Angel, and Hardy has been much attacked for the device by which the letter goes astray. It goes under the door and then under the carpet. But such mishaps do occur and when she discovers what has happened Tess still has the possibility of giving the letter to Angel. There is irony in Tess's belief, after the unfortunate incident in the town, that she and Angel will go a very long way away where 'no ghost of the past' can reach them, because the ghosts of the past d'Urbervilles and of the present pseudo-member of that family are everywhere, and are to be met again in the legend of the carriage and at Wellbridge Manor. It is as if Hardy is exploring the idea that we can never escape from our past. That the wedding day is New Year's Eve is significant in that it is now midwinter and the New Year marks the beginning of a new and tragic phase in Tess's life. And that tragedy is made all the more poignant by the observation that Angel 'did not know at that time the full depth of her devotion, its single-mindedness, its meekness; what long-suffering it guaranteed, what honesty, what endurance, what good faith'. Never has a woman's capacity for love been more finely described. Angel's love is, however, of a different sort, and Tess knows it: 'O my love, my love, why do I love you so . . . for she you love is not my real self, but one in my image'.

Chapter 34

Summary

Angel and Tess drive to Wellbridge to their lodgings in the farmhouse that had once been part of the Manor of a d'Urberville, and they immediately encounter another reminder of the past in the portraits on panels in the masonry of the two horrible-looking women who, centuries before, had been members of the d'Urberville family. A package is delivered to Angel from his father containing jewels which his godmother had left in trust for Angel's wife. Angel insists that Tess puts them on and declares how beautiful she is. Jonathan Kail arrives from Talbothays with their luggage with the news that Retty has tried to drown herself and Marian has 'been found dead drunk'. Tess in a fit of guilt feels she must tell all and is relieved when Angel tells her that he has a confession to make, he has indulged in 'eight-and-forty-hours dissipation with a stranger'. Tess sees this as the moment for her confession, not realising what the consequence will be, and she begins her story.

Commentary

The chapter brings the phase to a climax. Tess at last begins her confession and ends the suspense of the last few chapters. It is a supreme ironic stroke that Angel has a confession to make, too, and that Tess has no hesitation in forgiving him. She is, in fact, almost glad because now she is sure that he will forgive her, and she had had, after all, repeated assurances from Angel of his wish to protect her. At tea on that very day he had thought to himself 'And shall I ever neglect her, or hurt her, or even forget to consider her?' So little does he understand himself, so empty are all his fine thoughts! It is perhaps difficult for the reader to accept that the other milkmaids are driven to drink and near suicide by Angel's leaving the farm, but the point is used by Hardy to help bring Tess to the confession. By making Angel also guilty of a previous affair Hardy cleverly emphasises society's injustice in expecting different standards of men and women's sexual behaviour, and this may partly explain Angel's need to see Tess as a chaste angel. Hardy's observation that a peasant girl will become a beauty if clothed as a woman of fashion is a shrewd and sympathetic comment on life, and Tess's beauty is highlighted by the jewels she is given to wear, jewels which – ominously – give 'a sinister wink like a toad's' as she begins her confession, believing at last that because her affair was 'just the same' as Angel's all will be well.

3.5 PHASE THE FIFTH: THE WOMAN PAYS

Chapter 35

Summary

Tess ends her story and Angel cannot at first believe it. His reaction frightens Tess and she begs him to forgive her, but is rejected with bitterness. He tells her that 'the woman I have been loving is not you', and he accuses her of 'a want of harmony between your present mood of self-sacrifice and your past mood of self-preservation'. When he goes for a walk by himself she follows and begs him again to forgive her, but is met by bitterness and reproach and called 'the belated seedling of an effete aristocracy'. He sends her back home and she goes to her lonely marriage-bed while Angel eventually sleeps by himself in the sitting-room.

Commentary

This must be one of the most painful chapters in all literature. Angel's bitterness and cruelty to the woman he claimed to love are so skilfully developed that the reader shares Tess's sense of shock and her suffering, and we are left asking how can this educated man be so stupid, so unfair, so brutal? There is something of Othello in Angel in this chapter and even one or two echoes of the scene in which Desdemona is killed. And there is a terrible irony in his 'I don't wish to add murder to my other follies', because his behaviour will eventually lead to the murder of Alec. Even at these most personal and dramatic moments Hardy puts the action of his protagonists on to a cosmic scale by his description of the stars reflected in the pools of water in the road; 'the vastest things of the universe imaged in objects so mean'. Even now the first-time reader of the story might hope that Angel would take pity and accept the implication of his own 'You were more sinned against than sinning', but there are insistent forebodings. Angel, for example, is a black, sinister form as he walks beside Tess, and we are reminded of 'those shapes of darkness' which Tess had seen in the background of Talbothays and of those dark figures who will close in on her at Stonehenge. We are taken back to the beginning of the whole tragic sequence of events when Angel says, 'I think that the parson who unearthed your pedigree would have done better if he had held his tongue.'

Chapter 36

Summary

Angel wakes and calls Tess down to breakfast. He questions her about the baby and the 'man' and tells Tess that she is ignorant of the law when she suggests that he can divorce her. She tells him that she has considered suicide. Angel goes off to the mill each day and fights the temptation to respond to Tess's presence, and she is too good to use the wiles a woman of the world might have used. Angel becomes 'ill with thinking' and asks Tess, 'How can we live together while that man lives?' Finally, Tess suggests that she should leave him and go home, and Angel agrees as he has seen that it is advisable they should part.

Commentary

The agony of the honeymoon continues with a penetrating analysis of the mental and physical state of Angel: 'He was becoming ill with thinking; eaten out with thinking, withered by thinking.' The emphasis here on 'thinking' shows that Hardy is suggesting that Angel might be a better man if he responded more to his feelings, and Tess herself is appalled by her husband's will to subdue the flesh to the spirit. It is this twisted approach to his situation which makes him burst out with the question, 'How can we live together while that man lives?' and this undoubtedly plays its part in the final killing of Alec. Hardy, aware of his Victorian audience, tells us that 'Some might wish the odd paradox that with more animalism he would have been the better man' – a sentence not found in the serial version of the story – and then he adds, 'We do not say it'. If not, he certainly suggests it. And what a prig Angel shows himself to be when he bitterly complains that 'It isn't a question of respectability, but one of principle'! Compared with the knotted-up personality of Angel, Tess is comparatively straightforward. She continues to be loving, devoted and infinitely forgiving. As Hardy puts it, 'she sought not her own; was not provoked; thought no evil of his treatment of her'. Paradoxically, Tess becomes the saint, Angel the sinner, and by such means Hardy makes us question the whole basis of morality. There is another example of Hardy's prefiguring in that Tess thinks of committing suicide by strangling herself with the cord of her box.

Chapter 37

Summary

Angel goes sleep-walking, enters Tess's room, rolls her in a sheet 'as in a shroud', and carries her to the ruined Abbey-church where he lays her in an empty stone coffin. Tess cannot arouse him but, taking him by the arm, gets him back to the manor-house. Next morning he has no memory of the incident and Tess does not tell him. After breakfast they pack and leave by carriage, but have to call at the dairy where Tess suffers as they hide from Dairyman Crick and his wife what has happened on the honeymoon. Tess says goodbye to her favourite cows and then she and Angel set out again in the carriage. They part at a cross-road where Angel tells her that she is not to try to come to him, he will come to her if he can bring himself to bear it. He hands her a packet of money, puts her back in the carriage, and watches her driven away. When he turned to go his own way he 'hardly knew that he loved her still'.

Commentary

A great deal of irony is bound up with the words 'if only', and the reader is continually aware of the 'if onlys' in these chapters. If only Tess had not been so guilty and submissive; if only she had been willing to use her physical charms on him, and in this chapter, if only 'Tess had been artful, had she made a scene, fainted, wept hysterically . . . he would probably not have withstood her.' But she is, ironically, too good to take advantage of such means and Hardy also tells us something important about her character when he says that 'Pride, too, entered into her submission - which perhaps was a symptom of that reckless acquiescence in chance too apparent in the whole d'Urberville family.' Poignancy is present in the return to Talbothays where Tess had found a temporary happiness, and Hardy again emphasises the human situation through his description of nature when he writes, 'The gold of the summer picture was now gray, the colours mean, the rich soil mud, and the river cold.' And there is poignancy, and an insight into the disturbed state of Angel's mind, in the sleep-walking scene, even if there may be some difficulty in accepting its likelihood. Often, as here in 'When Tess had passed over the crest of the hill he turned to go his own way, and hardly knew that he loved her still', Hardy uses simple words in simple sentences to very powerful effect.

Chapter 38

Summary

Tess arrives back in Marlott and her mother calls her a 'little fool' for telling her husband about her past with Alec. Tess defends herself, and her mother breaks the news to Mr Durbeyfield when he comes in while Tess waits upstairs in a bedroom which has been so rearranged that there is no room for her. Her father's angry reaction to the news is such that after a few days Tess decides to leave home under the pretext that she is rejoining her husband, and she does so after giving her mother half of Angel's fifty pounds.

Commentary

The return to Marlott reminds the reader of the feckless background out of which Tess has grown and of her return from her unfortunate experiences at The Slopes. Her father still spends too much money at The Pure

Drop while boasting of his aristocratic connections. Tess's pitiful state is made worse by the way in which her parents receive her and it is clear that she is to find no consolation or understanding there. Her mother regards her as a fool, her father is so mortified that he even doubts whether Tess is really married. Once again, then, Tess finds herself forced to leave home, once again she travels the road.

Chapter 39

Summary
After nearly three weeks of travelling with a troubled heart, and wondering if he has treated Tess unfairly, Angel returns to his parents' home in Emminster to tell them that he has decided to emigrate as an agricultural-ist to Brazil. His mother and father find it strange that he has not brought his wife home but he makes an excuse. They question him about her: is she pretty, pure and virtuous? Was he her first love? At evening prayers they read the chapter in Proverbs about a virtuous wife, and with eyes 'full of tears' Angel goes off to his room. His mother, worried about him, follows and asks further questions about Tess, forcing him to describe her as 'spotless'. He blames Tess for forcing him into what he regards as a deceit.

Commentary
Angel's return to the parsonage at Emminster provides Hardy with the opportunity of examining yet further his agony of mind, while acquainting us with Angel's decision to go to Brazil. It may be thought that the irony is almost overdone in the questioning of Angel about the virtuousness of his wife and the reading of the Bible passage in praise of the virtuous wife, but the way in which he is forced into the utterance, 'She is spotless' is cleverly contrived, and Hardy's description of him as 'the slave to custom and conventionality' is a condemnation of all those who affect views in theory which do not last when confronted with reality. The description of Tess's hair as being like an immense rope again prefigures the manner of her death, while the sensuous reference to 'the velvet touch of her lips' is just one of very many allusions in the book to Tess's lips. They are part of her physicality which is an important element in the novel.

Chapter 40

Summary
Angel, still at Emminster, meets Mercy Chant and tries to shock her with his heterodox ideas. He prepares for his trip to Brazil and has to call at Wellbridge. Going up to the bedroom in which Tess had slept, he wonders

whether he has behaved generously and wisely. By chance he meets Izz
Huett and offers her a lift in his gig. They talk of the past, of Retty who
has gone into a decline and Marian who has taken to drink and been sacked
by the dairyman, and of the love of the dairymaids for Angel. Suddenly
he asks Izz to accompany him to Brazil and she agrees to do so even
though 'it will be wrong-doing in the eyes of civilization'. She loves Angel
very much but honestly admits that no one could love him more than
Tess did. Angel, ashamed of himself, withdraws his invitation and, although
deeply hurt, Izz forgives him before they part. Resisting the temptation
to go and find Tess, he takes the train for London and then leaves the
country.

Commentary

Angel's irresponsible behaviour in trying to shock Mercy Chant with his
fiendishly heterodox views - Hardy necessarily fails to tell us what they
were - and then his immoral proposal to Izz that she should accompany
him to Brazil, are devices used by Hardy to show us other facets of his
character. Hardy seems unable to forgive Angel for his treatment of Tess
and goes to almost extreme measures to reveal what a psychological case
he is. At this stage of the novel Angel is the embodiment of much that
Hardy is out to reveal as hypocritical, stupid, cruel and prejudiced. Narrow-
minded bigotry can be felt in the exchange between Angel and Mercy
Chant about Roman Catholicism, and there is something ludicrous, almost
laughable, in Mercy Chant's religious stance. A far more pagan culture is
associated with the mistletoe, for it was a sacred plant to the Druids, a
symbol of fertility, its berries being regarded as the semen of the gods.
Hardy makes good use of this symbol when Angel finds that the berries
of the mistletoe he had placed over the marriage-bed are now brown and
wrinkled. The contrast between Mercy Chant and Izz Huett is seen not
only in their names but in their characters. Mercy is almost too 'good'
to be true: Izz almost too true to be good. She loves Angel and would
'live in sin with him' but she cannot, even to help herself, lie about Tess's
love for him, and it is entirely appropriate that in a sentence that echoes
one of the great passages of the Bible, she says of Tess that 'She would
have laid down her life for 'ee.'

Chapter 41

Summary

It is an October day, more than eight months later. Tess has had some
work in the summer as a dairymaid but her money has almost gone, as
she had generously helped her family while hiding from them her own
penury. Meanwhile, in Brazil her husband is lying ill of fever. Looking for

work she hears from Marian that there is some available on an upland farm in the centre of the county. On the way there she is rudely accosted by the man who had been rude about her and had been knocked down by Angel. She runs away from him and hides in a plantation of trees. Her sleep is interrupted by thoughts of her husband and by strange flutterings and noises. In the morning she discovers that these come from shot pheasants who are lying about under the trees dying. She puts them out of their torture by breaking their necks.

Commentary

Tess has been identified with birds and other animals more than once in the novel, but in this chapter her sympathy with the suffering pheasants is a particularly striking instance of this, and she is, of course, herself described as 'a hunted soul'. She is suffering through man's cruelty and she, too, will have her neck broken. Our sympathy is won by her sympathy, and we become aware of a universal pattern of suffering and of man's cruelty not just to man but to animals as well. And, as Hardy points out, the pheasants are but 'weaker fellows in Nature's teeming family'. Once again, too, we are made aware of Tess's self-sacrificing kindness to her family. There is a very sharp contrast between Angel's behaviour in the previous chapter and Tess's in this, but both are now wanderers and once again we see Tess, like a pilgrim, travelling the road.

Chapter 42

Summary

Tess walks along the highway, and, finding herself commented upon by men, puts on one of her oldest field-gowns and nips off her eyebrows. The weather deteriorates and she arrives at her destination – Flintcomb-Ash – a place of stubborn soil where the labour required was of the roughest kind. She meets Marian who is shocked by her appearance and questions her about what has happened to her. She takes Tess to the farmhouse because it is pay-night and Tess is hired by the farmer's wife.

Commentary

Flintcomb-Ash in winter is to be an appalling contrast with Talbothays in summer, and Tess's mood and state are articulated by her environment. In this chapter we have a prelude to what is to come. Her external hardships are to mirror her internal distress. November has arrived, the weather becomes worse, the countryside around Flintcomb-Ash is bare, exposed and inhospitable. In Marian's words it is a 'starve-acre place', in Hardy's description 'sublime in its dreariness'. 'Thus Tess walks on' shows an interesting change to the present tense and briefly summarises what she has been doing almost throughout the story, with still no rest for her. Although her experience has taught her much about 'the cruelty of lust and the fragility of love' she still remains loyal to her husband and she harbours no ill-will. She now, significantly, wears her wedding-ring round her neck on a ribbon and her 'loneliness is excessive'. For Hardy, loneliness is often associated with tragedy.

Chapter 43

Summary
Tess and Marian work in a large, flint-covered field grubbing up turnips. They work on in the rain talking of happier days at Talbothays with Marian consoling herself from a pint bottle of spirits. Marian writes to invite Izz to join them at Flintcomb-Ash. Meanwhile winter comes with frost and snow and so bad is the weather that they have to work at reed-drawing in the barn. Here they find that Izz has arrived, and as they work together the farmer comes in and turns out to be no other than the man who had been rude to her at the inn and accosted her on the road. He decides to torment her to show who is master. Izz and Marian talk to her about Angel and Tess finds herself defending him but is very distressed when she hears from Marian of Angel's proposal to Izz that she should accompany him to Brazil.

Commentary
Various contrasts and conflicts are at work in this chapter: between Tess and Marian, between life at Talbothays and life at Flintcomb-Ash, and between Tess and the farmer. Hardy works on our sympathies for the two girls by showing the appalling conditions in which they have to work, and he shows us the essential neutrality of a Nature which can be so kind and benevolent in the Valley of the Great Dairies and so cruel and tyrannical in the swede-fields of Flintcomb-Ash. His admiration for the girls who work on 'hour after hour . . . not thinking of the justice or injustice of their lot' is one of the impressive features of a chapter which pays tribute to those who have to work under such conditions. One should particularly notice the sentence, 'But to stand working slowly in a field, and feel the creep of rain-water, first in legs and shoulders, then on hips and head, then at back, front, and sides, and yet to work on till the leaden light diminishes and marks that the sun is down, demands a distinct modicum of stoicism, even of valour'.

Chapter 44

Summary
Tess has been kept away from her in-laws by her sense of independence but now, worried by not having heard from Angel and by Izz's story, she decides to make the journey to Emminster. It is a year, all but a day, since the wedding. Her confidence decreases as she approaches her destination, but, leaving her thick working boots in the hedge and putting on her pretty, thin ones, she rings the doorbell of the vicarage, only to find that the whole family are at church. She meets the congregation coming out of the church, recognises Angel's two brothers, and overhears them talking about Angel's mistake in marrying a milkmaid. Then one of the brothers finds her boots and Mercy Chant goes off with them to give them to some poor person. Losing her confidence, Tess retreats without seeing Mr and Mrs Clare and starts on the journey back to Flintcomb-Ash. On her way she stops at Evershead for a drink of milk and learns that there is a 'ranter' preaching in the barn. Listening outside she becomes aware that the speaker describing his sins and his conversion is none other than her seducer, Alec d'Urberville.

Commentary
Once again Tess sets out on a journey, one which begins in hope but ends disastrously, and Hardy makes it clear that, although everything goes wrong for her, it is her 'loss of courage at the last and critical moment through her estimating her father-in-law by his sons' that is important. That is to say, Tess's character contributes to her troubles. But the reader may feel that in this chapter Hardy – if not the President of the Immortals – is having his sport with Tess. That she should arrive in Emminster just when Mr and Mrs Clare are in church is acceptable, but that she should overhear the odious brothers-in-law discuss her marriage, and that they should then discover her boots and go off with them, does rather strain one's credulity. And there is yet another and more disastrous coincidence: as a result of her failure of courage she arrives in Evershead just in time to meet the man 'who stood fair to be the blood-red ray in the spectrum of her young life', and – a supreme irony – Alec is now the converted preacher. Thus within a few hours she fails to meet the good preacher, Mr Clare, and meets the false preacher, Alec. As we enter a new phase of her story, affairs in her life are going from bad to worse and making her extremely vulnerable. It is difficult not to admire the brilliance of the structuring even if one is aware of how contrived it is.

3.6 PHASE THE SIXTH: THE CONVERT

Chapter 45

Summary
The sight of Tess has a devastating effect upon Alec, who chases after her, tells her how he was converted by no other than Mr Clare, and that he has now come to save Tess 'from the wrath to come'. Tess does not believe in his conversion. She tells him about the baby, and before leaving her he makes her swear on a pillar that he says was once a Holy Cross that she will not tempt him again. As she makes her way back she meets a shepherd who tells her that the 'Holy Cross' is, in fact, nothing of the kind: it marks the place of burial of a criminal.

Commentary
If one can accept the possibility of Alec the womaniser becoming Alec the preacher – and such conversions do take place – then one can admire the way in which Hardy extracts irony from the situation. Tess herself is conscious of 'the irony of the contrast' between Alec as she knew him and the Alec who now confronts her, and of the fact that 'He who had wrought her undoing was now on the side of the Spirit, while she remained unregenerate'. The greatest irony of all is, of course, that he should make her swear not to tempt him. The situation allows Tess to make some frank and courageous comments to Alec: 'You, and those like you, take your fill of pleasure on earth by making the life of such as me bitter and black with sorrow'. She does not believe in his conversion, and she is proved right. Would a genuine convert have had to say, 'Don't look at me like that', as if blaming her for being beautiful. No wonder poor Tess thinks that 'in inhabiting the fleshly tabernacle with which Nature had endowed her she was somehow doing wrong'. Could male chauvinism go further?

Chapter 46

Summary
Tess is working in the fields helping with the slicing of swedes when Alec comes to talk to her. Accepting the blame for the past, he produces a marriage licence and asks her to be his wife. He is disappointed when she tells him that she is already married and owns 'that the sight of you has waked up my love for you'. She tells him that Angel has deserted her and he leaves when Farmer Groby comes across to reprimand her for wasting time. That same night she writes to Angel declaring an undying affection but revealing a 'monstrous fear'. On a February day Alec comes to her lodgings to ask her to pray for him as he cannot get rid of her

image, and they have a discussion about Angel's beliefs. Alec's passion for Tess has caused him to miss a preaching engagement and Tess is blamed as a temptress. When he leaves her he ponders on the ironic fact that he has been influenced by the arguments against Christian dogmatism which he has heard from Tess's lips, and which she had heard from Angel.

Commentary

It is worth noting the power and economy with which the opening paragraph not only gives us a precise account of the way in which at that time swedes were sliced in a machine but also involves Tess with it. We have a visual picture, the 'swish' of the slicing-blades and the smell of the 'yellow chips'. In this chapter the threat to Tess grows as Alec decides that Tess is to be preferred to God, and there is poignancy in the letter she writes to her absentee husband. Alec has been repeatedly associated with the colour black, and he here appears as first a 'black speck' and then a 'man in black'. It is a redeeming feature in Alec that he is so prepared to marry Tess that he has obtained a marriage licence, and we learn more about Tess's stay at The Slopes when he refers to 'the whole unconventional business of our time at Trantridge'. Ironies abound in the religious discussion between Tess and Alec in which Tess does little more than repeat what Angel has told her, and irony is present in Alec's comment that 'that clever little fellow little thought that, by telling her those things, he might be paving my way back to her'. When Tess says that she believes 'in the *spirit* of the Sermon on the Mount' we are close to Hardy, who himself saw this as the essential part of Christianity, but there is irony, of course, in Tess's 'and so did my dear husband' because Angel has shown very little 'charity' in the treatment of his wife. Even Alec realises something of the true worth of Tess when he says, 'Why I did not despise you was on account of your being unsmirched in spite of all', and he here emerges as more sensitive and enlightened than Angel.

Chapter 47

Summary

It is March and the last wheat-rick at Flintcomb-Ash is being threshed. Tess is tried severely by the ceaselessness of the work and she is chosen by Farmer Groby for the most demanding job of all, supplying the man who feeds the drum of the threshing-machine with untied sheaves. Alec turns up and joins her as she eats her dinner. He accuses her again of having tempted him with her physical charms and they argue about ethics and dogma. Tess strikes Alec with her gauntlet when he calls Angel a mule, draws blood, and he goes off telling her that he was her master once, and will be again. The work on the threshing machine starts again.

Commentary

This chapter is concerned not just with Alec's further assault on Tess's feelings – to be contrasted with Angel's long wooing of her before the wedding – but with the harsh impact of modern mechanical methods on the old agricultural ways. Tess is under siege from the 'red tyrant' – the threshing-machine – and from the 'blood-red ray in the spectrum of her young life', Alec d'Urberville. The steam-engine which drives the threshing-machine is black and the morning air quivers with its 'hot blackness', while Alec has been repeatedly associated with darkness. The workers are under great strain as the 'inexorable wheels' spin and Tess's plight is made worse by the malice of Farmer Groby (also described as a 'tyrant') and the attentions of Alec. It is no wonder, then, that Tess, driven to the limit, bursts out with 'Once victim, always victim – that's the law!' We remember Magwitch in Charles Dickens's *Great Expectations*, who might have said just the same. Again Tess is compared to a bird as she looks at Alec 'with the hopeless defiance of the sparrow's gaze before its captor twists its neck', and Alec, all Christian charity now forgotten, tells her 'I was your master once! I will be your master again. If you are any man's wife you are mine.' The emphasis in that final sentence on their earlier sexual relationship is important as it provides a clue to the necessity Tess eventually feels to remove Alec before she can be fully Angel's wife. Her striking of Alec with the gauntlet so that 'the blood began dropping from his mouth upon the straw' is the angry response to his describing Angel as 'a mule', and it prefigures the final killing. As the chapter ends, Tess's plight seems desperate indeed. Will her husband return in time to save her?

Chapter 48

Summary

The painful work on the threshing-machine goes on and the farmer orders the workfolk to finish it that night. Alec remains on the scene, and Tess – shaken bodily by the spinning of the machine – keeps at work, frightened of being at the mercy of Alec if she loses her job. When work is at last finished she is so exhausted that Alec is able to get at her through his sympathy and his reference to her parents and sisters. In fear and despair she writes a long letter to Angel, describing herself as 'exposed to temptation' and begging him to come to her to save her from what threatens.

Commentary

Hardy tightens the noose, and exposes his heroine to such demands on her that she writes to her husband in a letter which is full of pathos. She could die in his arms, she lives entirely for him, and she is threatened by a danger she can only hint at. Hardy's authorial skill is seen at its best in the letter which reads so genuinely and tells us so much about Tess herself. She can reject Alec's cruder approaches to her but when he shows her and her family kindness she is very vulnerable, the more so when exhausted from the labours of the day. Tess is again compared to an animal, and this time it is Alec who compares her to a bled calf, and, of course, a calf was a sacrificial animal.

Chapter 49

Summary

Tess's letter is sent on to Angel in Brazil by his parents, who silently regret their treatment of him and are puzzled by his relationship with his wife. Meanwhile, Angel has been taken ill in Brazil where conditions for the English immigrants were appalling and many had died. His absence has mentally aged him a dozen years and given him the opportunity of questioning his views on morality. 'Who was the moral man? Still more pertinently, who was the moral woman?' He cannot understand why Tess does not write, not realising that she is just literally following his instructions to her. He meets another Englishman who tells Angel that he was wrong to leave Tess, and Angel becomes aware of his own inconsistencies and of his unfair treatment of her. His love for her is reborn and prepares him to be receptive to the letter which is on its way to him. Tess, meanwhile, tries to perfect the ballads which she knows Angel likes, so that she can sing them to him if he should return. Her fanciful dream is interrupted by the arrival of her sister, 'Liza-Lu, with the news that their mother is ill and dying. Tess decides that it is imperative to go home, and packs and leaves almost immediately.

Commentary

Hardy has to prepare us for the return of a reformed Angel and that process is begun in this chapter. Angel's illness and his meeting with the 'Englishman' have made him question his own behaviour and brought him round to see things very differently. Absence has made his heart fonder, and thoughts of his wedding and of Tess's devotion to him mean that 'from being her critic he grew to be her advocate'. Clare had been harsh towards her, Hardy says, but he then universalises the situation, making us see Clare's harshness to Tess, and implicitly our own individual harshness, as 'tenderness itself when compared with the universal harshness out of which they grow'. Tess's deviation from the social norm was insignificant, and what she 'had been was of no importance beside what she would be'. But while Angel in Brazil is slowly realising what a pearl he has thrown away, there is a serious development in England. The illness of her mother makes Tess decide in her usual altruistic way that she must give up her job and return home.

Chapter 50

Summary

Tess sets out in the darkness and, on arriving home, nurses her mother and organises the household arrangements. She also works on the family allotment and one March night while tending a bonfire she beholds the face of Alec looking at her as the fire flares up. He has come to see her, and he touches her in a weak place by telling her that he would like to help her brothers and sisters. She again rejects his assistance, but arrives home to find that her father has dropped dead, and his death means the end of the lease of their house.

Commentary

It is, of course, ironic that Tess comes home because her mother is ill, but it is her father who dies, taking with him their right to go on living in their old home. His death has been a possibility ever since Chapter 3, where Joan Durbeyfield tells Tess that her father has seen a doctor who has diagnosed heart trouble. Another example of retrospective reference occurs as Tess returns to Marlott and passes the very field in which she had danced but Angel had not danced with her. The pressure from Alec ·s now becoming intolerable, and he turns up by the bonfire like a devil with a steel-pronged fork. There is explicit symbolism here when, not for the first time in the novel, Tess is seen as Eve with Alec as the devil or 'Other One' come to destroy her. It is clear that Alec is not wholly bad, but he does represent evil, and Hardy's novel is very much about the clash between good and evil, between the exploited and the exploiters, between the pure and the impure.

Chapter 51

Summary

Cottage accommodation is much sought after in Marlott, and it is inevitable that the Durbeyfield family with their reputation for drunkenness and immorality should be turned out of their cottage. On the evening preceding their removal Tess sees herself as an evil influence in that her arrival home had contributed to their expulsion. Like a knight in armour, Alec rides up and offers his garden-house at Trantridge to the family but is told by Tess that they have taken rooms at Kingsbere, ancestral home and burial place of the d'Urberville family. Alec persists, telling her that he is positive Angel will never make it up with her. When he rides off, Tess, overcome by a sense of the injustice with which Angel has treated her, writes him a brief letter accusing him of cruelty and saying that she can never forgive him. On their last night in the old home the young children sing to Tess about Heaven, and she wishes that her own faith would enable her to 'leave them to Providence', but she lacks faith and it behoves her, therefore, to do something for them.

Commentary
Hardy writes with authority on the agricultural scene because he knows it well, and his opening paragraphs are an accurate description of the annual migrations from farm to farm which were destroying the old communities, and of the depopulation which he somewhat sadly sees as not so much what the statisticians call 'the tendency of the rural population towards the large towns' as 'the tendency of water to flow uphill when forced by machinery'. Tess's family is caught up in this process and their position is made worse by a moral condemnation which lacks any signs of charity. Now that her family is to be put out on the streets Tess feels increasingly responsible for them and even more at the mercy of the persistent Alec, who loses no opportunity to undermine her belief in Angel, and to put her in his debt by his kindness to those who are now dependent on her. And he understands Tess well enough to know that her pride will never allow her to appeal to her father-in-law. It is no wonder that Tess bitterly accuses her husband of monstrous treatment, and Hardy sees ghastly satire in Wordsworth's vision of a world into which we come 'trailing clouds of glory'.

Chapter 52

Summary
The hired waggon is loaded and the Durbeyfields leave Marlott. On the road they meet Marian and Izz who are also on the move, having decided they could no longer put up with Farmer Groby. When they arrive at Kingsbere they learn that their rooms have been let to someone else, and they are forced to unload the waggon under the church wall. The children are put to sleep in the four-post bedstead, and Tess's mother asks her, 'What's the use of your playing at marrying gentlemen, if it leaves us like this!' Alec arrives, again offering help, and Tess enters the church and looks at the tombs of her ancestors. He surprises her by lying on one of the tombs and tells her that he – the sham d'Urberville – can do more for her than 'the whole dynasty of the real underneath'. He leaves, and Tess wishes she were dead. Meanwhile, Marian and Izz, worried by Tess's predicament, write an anonymous letter to Angel telling him that his wife is 'sore put to by an Enemy in the shape of a Friend'.

Commentary

There is a fine description of 'house-ridding', the early morning start, the careful packing of the waggon, and the whole family under way with the cooking-pot swinging from the axle of the waggon. Tess's sense of guilt as her family find themselves homeless and sleeping in the churchyard leads her to wish that she were dead and puts her completely at the mercy of Alec. His comment that he, the sham d'Urberville, can do more for her than all her dead ancestors is a wry and ironic comment on the stupid snobbery of her father with his belief that being a descendant of the d'Urbervilles conferred some distinction on him. The final irony is that in the ancestral home of the d'Urbervilles Tess and her family find themselves homeless. In contrast with Alec's calculated attack on Tess we have the generosity of Izz and Marian who, alarmed by her condition, write to warn her husband that she is in great danger.

3.7 PHASE THE SEVENTH: FULFILMENT

Chapter 53

Summary

At Emminster Vicarage Mr and Mrs Clare wait anxiously for the return of Angel and, when he arrives, are shocked at how physically emaciated he is. He has received Tess's first letter, and her second awaits him. He writes to Marlott announcing his return and receives a reply from Mrs Durbeyfield telling him that they are no longer living in Marlott, that Tess is away from home and that she cannot give Tess's address. Then he decides that he must go in search of her, and, as he does so, the anonymous letter from Izz and Marian reaches him.

Commentary

Angel comes back into the story physically but it is a changed Angel, one whose emaciation causes his mother great distress, and provides Hardy with the opportunity of making one of those wise observations which add richness to the texture of the book: 'What woman, indeed, among the most faithful adherents of the truth, believes the promises and threats of the Word in the sense in which she believes in her own children, or would not throw her theology to the wind if weighed against their happiness?' Hardy has kept from his readers, and from Angel, just what has happened to Tess – we do not find out for another two chapters – so at this stage we know little more than Angel. Has she succumbed to Alec's insistent temptation? We do not know on our first reading. On our second reading we see the ironies in the situation and understand why Hardy's first title for the story was 'Too Late, Beloved'.

Chapter 54

Summary
Angel sets out on his search for Tess. He fails to find her at Flintcomb-Ash or Marlott, but at the latter he learns of the death of Jack Durbeyfield, finds his grave, and pays for the unpaid headstone. He traces Mrs Durbeyfield to her present home 'in a walled garden'. She refuses at first to give Angel Tess's address, but eventually in pity reveals that she is living somewhere in Sandbourne. He offers help to Mrs Durbeyfield but is told that they are 'fairly well provided for'.

Commentary
Hardy enriches his novels with a pattern of cross-references. In Chapter 1, Parson Tringham tells Jack Durbeyfield to chasten himself with the thought of 'How are the mighty fallen', and now in Chapter 54 we find those words on Jack's headstone. As Tess returns to her home in Chapter 50 she passes the field in which she had danced in Chapter 2, when Angel had not chosen her as a partner. Now in Chapter 54, Angel's 'way was by a field in which he had first beheld her at the dance'. The reader still doesn't know at this stage what has happened to Tess, but as her mother and sisters are living in 'a house in a walled garden', and as we know that Tess during her stay at Trantridge lived in a similar house, we can draw our own conclusions. Alec has provided Tess's family with accommodation and Tess is 'paying' for it; that this is so is made more certain by the embarrassment of Joan Durbeyfield as she is interrogated by Angel about Tess's whereabouts.

Chapter 55

Summary
Angel has arrived in Sandbourne and wonders where his cottage-girl wife could be 'amidst all this wealth and fashion'. From a postman he learns that there is a d'Urberville living at a stylish lodging-house called 'The Herons'. Early in the morning he calls there and the landlady says that she will see if Mrs d'Urberville is awake. Tess appears in a luxurious dressing-gown and he beseeches her to forgive him. Like someone in a dream she repeats, 'Too late, too late', and eventually he realises that she is living with Alec. She expresses her hatred for Alec because he had told her that Angel would never come back, and then Angel finds himself alone. He walks out into the street.

Commentary

A chapter of great dramatic intensity. It is entirely appropriate that Tess, who has become the mistress of Alec, should be found living in a stylish lodging-house and wearing an expensive cashmere dressing-gown. The shock the husband and wife feel as they recognise each other is powerfully but economically described. She, having believed Alec's words that Angel would never come back to her, stands like one in a dream, repeating 'Too late', and confused as to how much he understands the situation. He fails at first completely to understand Tess's state, and attributes her call to him to 'keep away' as revulsion at his emaciated condition. And when the truth does come through to him the situation is neatly summed up in 'Both seemed to implore something to shelter them from reality'. Significant details are Tess's 'cable' of dark-brown hair partly 'hanging' on her shoulder, Tess's expression of hatred for Alec, and Angel's recognition of a quality in Tess that has been mentioned before – her ability to withdraw her spirit from her body, so that the body drifts like 'a corpse upon the current in a direction dissociated from its living will'.

Chapter 56

Summary

Mrs Brooks, the landlady, is curious about the events she has just witnessed. She listens outside the door of the apartment which has been taken by the d'Urbervilles and hears Tess moaning in her distress. She accuses Alec of using 'cruel persuasion upon her', of having lied to her, and, as a result she has lost Angel for a second time and her life is torn all to pieces. The landlady hears sharp words from 'the man' and the sudden rustle as Tess springs to her feet. Frightened of being caught, Mrs Brooks hastily retreats downstairs. After finishing her breakfast she sees Tess leaving the house, and then later, leaning back in her chair, she sees a red spot in the ceiling. It grows in size until it has the appearance of a 'gigantic ace of hearts'. Frightened, she calls in a workman who finds Alec dead in bed. He has been stabbed with a carving-knife. The news of the murder soon spreads.

Commentary

It is inevitable that Alec must die if Tess is to be able to regard Angel as completely her husband, and this is the murder scene. Hardy handles it extremely well. As in a Greek tragedy we do not see the killing but have it described after it has occurred. Its horror is conveyed by the red stain on the ceiling and the 'Drip, drip, drip' of blood on to the floor. We are told that 'the point of the blade had touched the heart of the victim', and we are reminded of the death of Prince, the horse, in Chapter 4 when the 'pointed shaft of the cart had entered the breast of the unhappy Prince

like a sword' and how Tess was splashed with blood and thought of herself as a murderess. Again we meet card imagery in the description of
the bloodstain on the ceiling as being like a 'gigantic ace of hearts'. The
passages of dialogue overheard by Mrs Brooks reveal Tess's desperate state
at the realisation that she seems to have lost Angel for the second time,
and 'her lips were bleeding from the clench of her teeth upon them'.
The end of this chapter was the end of an instalment of the serial, and
the reader was left wondering where Tess has gone and what fate awaits
her.

Chapter 57

Summary
Like a sleepwalker, Angel returns to his hotel, has breakfast, and leaves
for the station. Tess runs after him and tells him that she has killed Alec.
She asks Angel to forgive her sin against him now that she has killed the
other man. Angel doesn't know whether to believe her story, but tells
her that he will protect her by every means in his power. They walk on,
avoiding high roads, and in the depths of the New Forest they find a
mansion called Bramshurst Court which is uninhabited as it is to be let
furnished. Angel discovers that there is only an old woman in charge as a
caretaker who comes from a nearby hamlet on fine days to open and shut
the windows, and he and Tess take refuge in the house.

Commentary
Tess and her beloved Angel are together again in search of a brief fulfilment before the forces of the Law catch up with Tess. By allowing the
couple to spend a few days together, Hardy adds immeasurably to the
pathos of these closing chapters. It enables Tess to pour out her feelings
to Angel. Alec had done wrong not just to her but to Angel as well, and
her request that Angel will forgive her sin against him now that Alec is
dead shows just how inevitable the murder was. At first Angel doubts
what Tess is telling him, but, ironically enough, as the truth of her story
is borne in on him, 'Tenderness was absolutely dominant in Clare at last',
and he swears to protect her by every means, and we are reminded of an
earlier occasion before the wedding when he told her, 'I don't like you to
be left anywhere away from my protection and sympathy'. He has come a
long way since then. So hopeless is the situation that the plans they make
are 'like the plans of two children', and there is something appropriate in
the fact that they should spend their first night together in a country
mansion. Throughout the chapter, however, there are indications of the
future. The boughs are 'moaning' among the fir-trees, they sit down

'upon some dead boughs', and the chapter ends 'they were enveloped in the shades of night which they had no candle to disperse'.

Chapter 58

Summary
They are left undisturbed in the mansion for six blissful days. Tess is so happy that she is unwilling to leave. Then on the next morning the care-taker arrives to open the windows and, discovering them sleeping, goes off to consult her neighbours. Waking soon after in a disturbed state Angel decides that they must leave. They pass near Melchester and in the dark of night reach a 'monstrous place' which Angel recognises as Stonehenge. Tess flings herself upon an 'oblong slab' which turns out to be the altar of sacrifice. They talk for a while and Tess asks Angel to marry 'Liza-Lu 'if anything happens to me'. She falls asleep, dark figures approach, and Angel realises that there is no escape. In response to Angel's plea they allow her to sleep on. She awakens in the 'growing light' and announces herself ready to be taken away.

Commentary
If we see Tess as symbolic of deceived and abused women and we remember the many associations of Angel with the sun it is completely appropriate that Tess should make her final appearance in the novel lying like a sacri-fice on the altar-stone of an ancient religion which worshipped the sun. This may be regarded by some readers as too contrived, but for many Tess is such a real person and there is such authenticity in the description of the scene that it is a completely acceptable and brilliantly conceived con-clusion to Tess's life. During her short but happy honeymoon she achieves a fulfilment so complete that she is loath to leave and there is significance in her final words 'This happiness could not have lasted . . . I am ready'. We are reminded of Hamlet's, 'The readiness is all', and made to consider the possibility that fulfilment can often only be achieved by suffering. Their honeymoon-house, so different from Wellbridge, becomes a symbol of 'affection, union, error forgiven' while 'outside was the inexorable'. Most of us have experienced at the end of some great happiness this feeling of life and time's inexorability. As they approach Stonehenge there is an emphasis on darkness and on 'black', a colour which has been used for its metaphorical associations throughout the book. The night grows 'as dark as a cave', something makes 'the black sky blacker', the mono-liths and trilithons are 'blackly defined' and the dark figures which converge upon Stonehenge and its sacrifice remind us of the darkness frequently associated with Alec, and of those 'shapes of darkness' she knew to be in the background even when she was at Talbothays (Chapter 31). Tess, with

her care for 'Liza-Lu, her deep and spiritual love for Angel, and her brave and wise comments on her feelings and her situation, emerges in this remarkable chapter as one of the great tragic heroines of English literature.

Chapter 59

Summary
Angel and 'Liza-Lu leave Wintoncester prison and climb the great West Hill. The clocks strike eight and they see a black flag slowly move up the staff fixed upon the cornice of the prison tower. They bend in prayer and 'As soon as they had strength they arose, joined hands again, and went on.'

Commentary
There is a strikingly different tone about this final short chapter. It is detached, almost austere, as if Hardy was determined to keep the emotional level low. Classical and Shakespearean tragedy almost always concluded – after the catastrophe – with a dying fall: in John Milton's words, 'With calm of mind/All passion spent'. Tess's tragedy had come to its moving, and in some ways triumphant, end with her 'I am ready'. But Hardy needs to record her death by hanging, and this he does in an almost matter-of-fact way. There is a brief picture of Wintoncester 'in all the brightness and warmth of a July morning', and then we are told of the 'two persons', only later identified as Angel and 'Liza-Lu, making their way up the hill. And even now, on our first reading, we are not sure of the exact meaning of all this. But eight o'clock sounds from the clocks in the town, and the 'paralyzed suspense' of the two persons makes it certain that this is the moment of Tess's death. The gaze of the couple, and of the readers, is gradually directed to the 'ugly flat-topped octagonal tower . . . the one blot on the city's beauty'. And the raising of the 'black flag' tells us that, in Hardy's ironic words ' "Justice" was done'. The following words, 'the President of the Immortals, in Aeschylean phrase, had ended his sport with Tess', seem to suggest that Tess had been fated from the beginning, but Hardy denied this, claiming that 'it was no more than a trope [figurative expression] indicative of the way the fate of Tess impresses unreasoning humanity'. Tess's fate has been brought about partly by chance, partly by her own character, but this is true of all great tragic figures, and we weep that this should be so. The very last sentence is powerfully simple and direct, and is an echo of the description of Adam and Eve as they leave Paradise in Milton's *Paradise Lost*.

4 WHAT THE NOVEL IS ABOUT

When *Tess* was first published it had an immediate success and it has remained a 'best-seller' ever since. To enjoy such popularity with a wide audience requires one particular quality: it must have the ability to entertain. But that in itself would not have ensured its survival over a hundred years. Even if we read it primarily for the pleasure of reading, we cannot fail to be aware that *Tess* is a serious novel, that is to say, it is packed with ideas about life, and this is one of the elements of its greatness. Hardy wanted to write a novel which would entertain (in fact, he needed to do so if it was to sell well and earn him his living!), but because he was passionately interested in human relationships he poured into his novels impressions of life as he saw it. Thus, he was conscious of the hypocrisy of those who had one moral standard for men and another for women, and this becomes an important aspect of *Tess*.

The England in which Hardy had grown up had been an England of rigid moral codes and very dogmatic ideas about the relationships between men and women. He found himself increasingly questioning the assumptions of the time and the attitudes of the Church which imposed them. In *Tess* there is little sympathy for Parson Tringham who - ironically and significantly - triggers off the whole unhappy story by his disclosure to 'Sir John' of his ancestral heritage, and there is nothing but contempt for Angel's two insufferable brothers. There is also powerful criticism of the Vicar of Marlott who has 'the natural feelings of a tradesman at finding that a job he should have been called in for had been unskilfully botched by his customers'. What kind of religion is it, Hardy is asking, which would condemn to damnation a baby who had not been baptised or visit the sins of the father on the child. Hardy sees some good in the evangelical Parson Clare and his wife, but we may take it that he intends there to be something amusing and paradoxical in their deep interest in Tess as soon as they learn that she is a 'sinner'.

For Hardy, Tess is not, of course, a sinner, and he nailed his colours to the mast when he decided to add to the title the challenging words 'A

Pure Woman'. It is worthwhile thinking very deeply about this move of Hardy's. He was bitterly attacked for calling Tess 'pure', and the Establishment of the 1890s found *Tess* a very disturbing book. Purity meant chastity, and a woman must before all else be chaste. Virginity was all-important. Hardy, who had been brought up in the country and was so sensitively aware of the power of Nature, questioned this. He knew that among the workers in the fields there was not the same emphasis on virginity, and that what happened between Alec and Tess did not condemn her to be a perpetual moral outcast. Tess has 'been made to break an accepted social law, but no law known to an environment in which she fancied herself such an anomaly'. Hardy seems to be saying, 'Why make the physical act itself a matter of such paramount importance?'

Tess's problem is that she stands between two cultures, that of her parents and her natural surroundings, and that which has resulted from her having 'passed the Sixth Standard in the National School'. This is to some extent Hardy's own problem because he himself is an educated man from a humble background and a country environment, and in his novels he shows himself preoccupied by the difficulties confronting those who find themselves, like Tess, caught between two worlds, the old and the new. Hardy is aware of the 'ache of modernism' and his sympathies are with the old world, the world of his youth untouched by new ideas and new technology, the arguing of theologians and the mobility provided by trains and improved transport, but he knows, too, that progress brings its benefits, and he makes his ambivalent attitude on this issue very clear in his essay 'The Dorsetshire Labourer'.

Tess finds herself critical – although loyally supportive – of her family and yet her background makes her not easily acceptable to Angel's middle-class family. She is, therefore, doubly a figure in transition – she is caught between two classes and between two moral codes. Her plight is brought home to us by the fact that she has no permanent home throughout most of the novel. She seems to be continually travelling, forever setting out on the road to somewhere or other, and her unsettledness of mind is reflected in her constant movement from one place to another. And, of course, she is unlucky in that her travels bring her into contact with two men who represent two powerful forces which between them will destroy her.

Alec can be seen as representative of the cruelty of lust, Angel of the fragility of love. Even if Hardy seems to be saying that there is nothing naturally sinful in the sexual act or sacred in virginity, not for a moment does he condone Alec's treatment of Tess. He is a bully who uses his money and his position to master and exploit women. He takes advantage of Tess's innocence and vulnerability, and such a relationship is seen by Hardy as wholly deplorable. The blame is put by him on the exploiter and not the exploited, and it is in this that he throws a challenge down to

Victorian society with its 'fallen women' and its belief that all such women must be impure and should be unhappy. Their illegitimate offspring, it was tacitly accepted, should be labelled bastards and ought to die at birth or soon after. Hardy follows the conventional pattern in making his heroine unhappy, letting her baby die, and bringing her to a tragic end, but he will not have it that her experience with Alec must coarsen her and make her 'impure'.

Her unhappiness is partly the result, as we have already said, of her education which has developed her sense of sin and guilt, but it is far more the result of failures in Angel, the man who claims to love her. He is a far more complex figure than Alec. Where Alec is a pseudo-gentleman and a pseudo-d'Urberville, Angel is a pseudo-liberal and a pseudo-angel. With his interest in 'intellectual liberty' and his condemnation of 'an untenable redemptive theolatry' he seems a man of the broadest outlook who would be able to love Tess for what she is, the kind of man who might well ask, 'Who was the moral man? Still more pertinently, who was the moral woman?' But on his wedding night he shows himself to be narrow-minded and as bound by Victorian orthodox morality as the most puritanical bigot, a fault made worse by his own confession to Tess of a previous sexual misdemeanour, and his unquestioning acceptance of a double standard of behaviour. Hardy savagely enjoys himself exposing Angel's weaknesses, which he sees as those of a cruel and insensitive society. That such a potential for happiness and fulfilment should be destroyed by Angel indicates what is wrong with society: the word has become more important than the spirit.

Angel's rejection of Tess illustrates yet another of Hardy's recurring themes: the dangers of idealisation, of living in a dream world. Love is for him a 'great thing', and nowhere in literature is love between man and woman more beautifully and powerfully described than in the Talbothays chapters of *Tess*. However, it is vital for happiness that one should love the person and not the idea. Angel thinks that he loves Tess but much of his love is linked to his idea of what Tess is. Almost his first thought about her is, 'What a fresh and virginal daughter of Nature that milkmaid is!', and he continually sees her as 'a visionary essence of woman', as the Greek goddess of chastity, and as being 'chaste as a vestal'. He is so obsessed by this physical idea of purity, possibly because of guilt feelings brought about by his own fall from sexual grace, that it is no wonder that he is able to say to the distressed Tess on their wedding night, 'the woman I have been loving is not you'. How right Tess is when she tells him, 'It is in your own mind what you are angry at, Angel; it is not in me'! It is a measure of Angel's conversion that he is able finally to accept her as a murderess when earlier in the book she had been rejected for a small sexual indiscretion. Hardy uses him here to explore the idea that the nineteenth-century Church puts its emphasis far too much on the physical and far too little on loving-kindness, far too much on chastity, too little on charity. Religion has become a rigid orthodoxy, out of touch with reality, a situation nicely summed up in the description of Angel's brothers as being unable to see 'the difference between local truth and universal truth'. It will be seen that criticism of religious and social codes permeates the whole novel.

Tess finds herself in conflict with these codes and through her Hardy explores yet another area of life which fascinates him – the relationship between character and fate. It is often said that Tess is doomed from the beginning of the novel, and it is certainly true that there is a feeling of tragic inevitability. However, it is indisputable that Tess's character affects the action of the story. Her terrible sense of guilt, her dithering about telling Angel of her past, her pride which makes her leave Emminster without seeing her mother and father-in-law, all these play their part in her tragedy. What each reader must consider is the extent to which Tess's character is her fate. Does she have to behave as she does? Where she has a choice does she have to make the one she does? Of course, chance plays a part, and it is a common criticism of Hardy's novels that chance plays too big a part. The example often quoted from *Tess* is that of the confessional letter written by Tess to Angel going under the carpet. But he might have argued that this kind of bad luck does happen in life, and he does remark on 'that reckless acquiescence in chance too apparent in the whole d'Urberville family'. When Tess discovers that Angel has not read her letter she could still have handed it to him before the wedding. Isn't life, he might have said, a mixture of character and chance and haven't I got the mixture just about right in *Tess*? What do *you* think?

These are some of the major ideas which make *Tess* such a rich novel. But there are many other ideas because Hardy had so lively a mind, such deep feelings, and so great an interest in life, that his books, as we have already seen, are a constant commentary on life. Heredity became a serious study about the time he was writing *Tess*, and it is very much present in the story which begins, of course, with Jack Durbeyfield's learning about his ancestors, and which refers more than once to what Tess may have inherited from her aristocratic predecessors. We are also made aware of what Tess has inherited from her mother and father. It is worth looking in detail at this aspect of the novel, and others which would well repay study are superstition and the treatment of animals. Hardy leaves no doubt where he stands on the latter. In a post-Darwinian world he thinks of animals as being related to us, and man's inhumanity to animals he sees as only slightly less culpable than man's inhumanity to man. There is a peculiar poignancy, an ironic aptness, about Tess's putting the dying pheasants out of their agony by breaking their necks, and she is herself repeatedly compared to animals. About superstition, Hardy's attitude is more ambivalent. What are we to make of *The Compleat Fortune-Teller*, of the legend of the d'Urberville coach, and the cock crowing in the afternoon? Does Hardy include them because of the colour they add to his story or because he knows that superstition plays some part in most people's lives and it is, therefore, a matter of concern? Hardy's novels always give one a great deal to think about, and that is one reason for their lasting appeal.

5 TECHNICAL FEATURES

5.1 THE STORY AND ITS STRUCTURE

In the rural environment of Hardy's youth the telling of stories and anecdotes was an important part of life, and he heard many a tale from his grandmother, his parents, relatives and friends. Some of these he made notes of for future use, and he was always looking for incidents which he could use in his books. Thus, he claimed that he had actually heard a tipsy man swaggering past him and singing 'I've-got-a-great-family-vault-over-at . . . ' and that the death of Prince, the horse, and the bloodstained ceiling were based upon actual newspaper reports. Brought up in this tradition, he couldn't understand a novelist like Henry James who seemed to him to write books in which very little happened. For Hardy, a story should be exceptional enough to justify its telling: 'We tale-tellers are all Ancient Mariners,' he wrote, 'and none of us is warranted in stopping Wedding Guests (in other words, the hurrying public) unless he has something more unusual to relate than the ordinary experience of every average man and woman'.

Although it has become fashionable in some critical circles to sneer at the story as being the least valuable part of a book, it could be claimed that it is Hardy's ability as a story-teller which has played a large part in his popularity as a novelist. The story of Tess is a good one. It makes excellent use of suspense, surprise and irony. As it was first conceived as a serial, it is packed with dramatic incidents of a vividness which makes them stand out in the memory when the general outline of the plot is forgotten. By Victorian standards the plot is, in fact, comparatively simple. A country girl is forced by poverty to go out to work for a moneyed family; she is seduced by the son of the house, but leaves him when she finds herself pregnant; the baby dies and she goes off to work as a dairy-maid. She falls in love with a middle-class man who is training to be a farmer. He declares his love for her and asks her to marry him. She feels that she should tell him about her seduction but fails to do so until the wedding night, when he angrily rejects her. Leaving her, he goes off to Brazil and she, after working in appalling conditions and in order to save her poverty-stricken family, becomes the mistress of the man who originally seduced her. Her husband has a change of heart, returns from Brazil, and eventually traces her. She kills the seducer and has a few brief days of happiness with her husband before she is captured and hanged.

Put thus it seems a simple, elemental plot on the common subject of the seduced maid and her sufferings, but Hardy transforms it through the power of his creative imagination, loading it with interesting characters and memorable descriptions, and continually challenging our normal expectations and responses to this conventional seduction story. Unusually, he divides the book into 'Phases': in the first phase she is 'The Maiden', the young, virginal girl so vulnerable to such as Alec, whose seduction of her means that in Phase the Second she is 'Maiden No More', and we are able to observe the effect on her life of that seduction, of her brief motherhood, and of the death of her child. The third phase of her life is 'The Rally' which occurs when, having seemingly recovered from her early misfortunes, she sets out for the dairy-farm in the spring and, in hope, meets Angel, and knows a brief happiness as they fall in love. In such a lush and benevolent atmosphere as that of Talbothays in the summer we feel, surely, all must be well, but Phase the Fourth, 'The Consequence' shows the shadows growing as winter approaches and, as a consequence of her seduction, Tess worries herself to distraction about her guilty secret. Just as Phase the First ends with her loss of virginity, Phase the Fourth ends with her marriage and the arrival of the moment of confession. 'The Woman Pays', the title of Phase the Fifth has been carefully chosen because it puts the emphasis on 'The Woman'. It is not Alec or Angel but the *woman* who pays, and she will continue to pay until that moment when she becomes the supreme sacrifice. Phase the Fifth ends almost ironically with her meeting the 'converted' Alec, an event which far from ending her paying will only add to it, and it must have been with some further irony that Hardy entitled Phase the Sixth 'The Convert'. In it Alec 'progresses' from convert to sinner, or to put it another way, suffers a further conversion at the hands of Tess who uses Angel's criticism of organised religion in order to restore him to his previous state. Meanwhile Angel is being 'converted' through his experiences in Brazil, and it is he who introduces Phase the Seventh, 'Fulfilment', by returning to England after his calamitous absence from the scene throughout Phase the Sixth. The title 'Fulfilment' is ambiguous. Angel and Tess have their romantic fulfilment for a few days at Bramshurst Court, but the title could also be taken to refer ironically to what happens to Alec or even to Tess's final fate. Such ambiguities add a richness to the book's texture.

The structure of the novel depends, then, upon the seven phases, but Hardy adds to this by building up a pattern of references and cross-references which resonate through the story. Thus when Tess impulsively hits Alec's face with her leather glove, and when she kills him, we are reminded of Parson Tringham's, 'However, our impulses are too strong for our judgement sometimes'. When we hear the legend of the d'Urberville coach we are reminded of Jack Durbeyfield riding home in a carriage after hearing the news of his aristocratic connections in Chapter 1. And as the hour strikes eight and Tess dies in the final chapter we think of another clock striking in Chapter 3, 'when suddenly the student said that he must leave'. It is rewarding to look for the many other instances of this patterning which add so much to our feeling that this is a very carefully structured novel.

In talking about structure we should also bear in mind Hardy's cosmic view of his story, his ability suddenly to change the perspective. For most of the time we are concerned with characters who seem to be real people living in a minutely observed world. We see and hear the scene in the field when the reaping of the wheat is taking place, and it is described in such vivid detail that we are present ourselves. At Talbothays the dairy farm and the milkers are so presented that a whole way of life at a particular time is immortalised. We are told of the methods of milking, of the difficulties which can arise, and of the day's activities. We even know the names of the cows, and we can see the long, thatched sheds and the eaves supported by wooden posts. It is all so lifelike, so present, so touchable – and then Hardy adds that these posts have been 'rubbed to a glossy smoothness by the flanks of infinite cows and calves of bygone years, now passed to an oblivion almost inconceivable in its profundity', and we see the situation from a wholly different perspective. Hardy's cosmic view frames his story, making us aware from time to time of our own littleness in the perspectives of time and space. As Tess walks to Talbothays she is suddenly portrayed 'like a fly on a billiard-table of indefinite length, and of no more consequence to the surroundings than that fly'. By such means Hardy not only structures his novel but also adds to its meaning. We are united by our common humanity. We exist as individuals but are united by the passing of time and the inevitability of death.

5.2 CHARACTERISATION

Tess herself is central to the novel and Hardy describes her with such a wealth of physical detail and comment upon her thoughts and feelings that we feel that we know her well. It has been said that Hardy fell in love with his own creation, that he shares her sufferings as a father might those of his daughter, and this is undoubtedly true. He several times mentions her fluty voice and her well-developed figure. There are constant references to her lips, and Angel thinks of these as being 'distracting, infatuating, maddening'. Her lips and teeth remind him of the old Elizabethan simile of 'roses filled with snow', and Alec tries to force a strawberry between her parted lips. To Angel her lips are not quite perfect, 'And it was the touch of the imperfect upon the would-be perfect that gave the sweetness, because it was that which gave the humanity'. Writing when he did, Hardy has to be very careful in writing about the physical aspect of love but he leaves us in no doubt about Tess's physicality and her sexual attraction to men.

But it is her character, of course, that is so important to the story, and as an answer to the uncharitable who would see Tess as a wicked sinner, Hardy makes her almost a human angel, 'with a touch of the imperfect'. Yes, of course, she is proud, occasionally impulsive, and sometimes too passive, but what a long catalogue of virtues may be set against these occasional faults! Our love of her and sympathy for her are partly caused by our awareness of her loyalty and devotion to her feckless family. It is for them that she first goes to Trantridge and finally becomes Alec's mistress. We are bound to feel sympathy for a sixteen-year-old girl who already finds herself having to get her parents back from their drinking at the alehouse and doing the work which her impossible father should be doing. She has a great love for her brothers and sisters, and love is what we most remember her for. The compassion she feels for the wounded pheasants and her love for her special cows identify her with the nature of which she is a part, and she becomes representative of the best of that nature. We see her, too, as a mother trying at first to hide the love she feels for that poor baby, Sorrow, but then passionately revealing it in her anxiety about her baby's illness, about his christening, and about his burial. But it is the quality of her love for Angel which is her special mark of distinction, just as it is Hardy's distinction as a great writer that he can portray such love. It is a love which is both physical – 'Clare learnt what an impassioned woman's kisses were like upon the lips of one whom she loved with all her heart and soul' – and emotional, and also has something of the spiritual about it. When Hardy writes of Angel not knowing 'at that time the full depth of her devotion, its single-mindedness, its meekness; what long-suffering it guaranteed, what honesty, what endurance, what good faith' he is deliberately echoing a famous passage in the Bible in which St Paul talks about Christian love, and he does so not just to shock the orthodox into considering the true nature of love, but also because Tess's love has something heavenly about it.

Described in such detail and with so much love, Tess is superbly real and living, and yet there is an important sense in which she is far more than Tess the milkmaid. Part of Hardy's object in writing the novel, as we have already said, was to expose how badly women could be treated sexually under a moral code which favoured the male. To make his point as strongly as possible he creates Tess to be both individual and symbol. We see this first in Chapter 7 where Tess sets out to take up residence at The Slopes, and there are repeated indications that she is being sacrificed by her mother and father – her hair is washed, she is dressed in white, the family group is 'a picture of honest beauty flanked by innocence', and she is carried away to her fate by Alec. As a field-woman she is a 'portion of the field'. Fighting for her baby's salvation at the baptism, she is seen by her brothers and sisters as 'a being large, towering, and awful', while she is more than once compared to Eve, the mother of all women, and Angel sees her as 'a visionary essence of woman'. The result of this is that when Tess lies on the sacrificial stone at Stonehenge at the end of her painful pilgrimage through life most readers have no difficulty in accepting what might otherwise have seemed too contrived an incident. At this stage she becomes more symbol than individual and for this Hardy's careful planning has prepared us.

Tess so dominates the novel, which very properly is given her name as a title, that the other characters must seem minor by comparison. There *is* something of the cardboard villain about *Alec* with his swarthy complexion, black moustache with curled points and bold, rolling eye. And, of course, he smokes! He is continually associated with darkness and there are parallels drawn between him and the Devil. To that extent he is a symbol of evil, and Hardy who has made him so is not as successful in combining symbol and individual in Alec as he is in Tess. The Alec who seems to be so devoted to Tess that he is prepared to marry her, even if much of the attraction is physical, is a little difficult to reconcile with the demonic Alec who, complete with steel-pronged fork, digs by her in the allotment until his face is lit up by the fire.

It may be difficult to accept his conversion, except as further evidence of the failure of the Church, and as a narrative device which enables Hardy to draw the maximum of irony from his 'un-conversion', but it is a well-known psychological fact that passionate sinners can become passionate religious converts. Certainly, it allows Hardy to set Tess's faith in a 'religion of loving-kindness and purity', (and it is worth thinking carefully about what she means by 'purity' there) against Alec's statement that 'I am not going to feel responsible for my deeds and passions if there's nobody to be responsible to'. Appropriately, Alec is an outsider in the rural community – his father has made his money 'as an honest merchant (some said money-lender) in the North' - and even his name is false. His generosity to Tess's family results from his belief that money can buy anything, and it is significant that in Chapter 12 he says, 'I am ready to pay to the uttermost farthing' and his words to Tess are echoed by her in Chapter 34 where Tess, having decided to tell Angel of her relationship with Alec, says to herself that she will 'pay to the uttermost farthing', but whereas Alec's words are literal, he is thinking in terms of money, Tess's words are metaphorical - and both of them do pay to the uttermost farthing. Alec has so much money, Tess so little, and it is the moneyed man who says, 'I was born bad, and I have lived bad, and I shall die bad in all probability'. With his selfishness, his bad temper and his desire to master not only his horses but his women, there is much to dislike about Alec, but we should remember that Tess does find it possible to say of him, 'My eyes were dazed by you for a little', and 'perhaps you are a little better and kinder than I have been thinking you were'. Perhaps Hardy himself was a little puzzled at what to make of his playboy of the Wessex world.

Angel is a far more complex character although he is like Alec in that he may be seen as the outsider who has come into the rustic community, and, like him, he treats Tess shabbily. It could even be argued that he is crueller and more callous than Alec in that he claims to love Tess, whereas Alec never makes quite the same protestations of affection and caring. Angel is an interesting character in that his views about the dogmatism of the Church resemble closely views that we know Hardy to have held. He sees himself as an intellectual rebel, questioning the conventions of the time, and liberal in outlook. Sexually he seems somewhat inconsistent. He is deeply sensitive to Tess's physical charms and has had, almost unbelievably - even though it is necessary for Hardy to make his point about double standards - a short sexual encounter before he meets Tess. Yet he is able to reject Tess on the wedding night, beautiful as she is. In a roundabout way Hardy suggests that it might have been better if he had had a little more 'animalism' about him, but the invitation to Izz to accompany him to Brazil smacks more of 'animalism' than love. Whether these inconsistencies are a weakness resulting from Hardy's need to make a point or whether they are acceptable as the kind of inconsistency we find in characters in real life must be decided by the individual reader.

Although in his attitude to the Church Angel may seem to speak for his creator, when he fails to live up to his own beliefs and treats Tess so badly on their honeymoon Hardy's contempt for him is manifest. How could he be so hypocritical, so vicious in his attack on Tess, so insensitive to her devotion to him! But Hardy is shrewd and experienced enough to know that men and women are often in love with the ideal rather than the real, that there is often a gap between ideas and feelings, between one's beliefs and one's behaviour. The liberal Angel becomes a puritanical reactionary when he finds that his wife is not a virgin, and it takes a severe illness and a period in Brazil for him to ask the vital question, 'Who was the moral man? Still more pertinently; who was the moral woman?'

Interestingly and ironically, while Angel is abroad suffering his conversion, Tess at home takes over the 'religion of loving-kindness' which he had preached to her and preaches it to Alec. When we meet Angel again in England he is much changed both physically and mentally, at last a true believer in the ideas he had betrayed on his wedding-night. The love he now shows to Tess is all-understanding but it has come too late. Just as Alec is identified with darkness, Angel is repeatedly associated with the sun. When he leaves Marlott in Chapter 3 'the rays of the sun had absorbed' his retreating figure; when there is talk of his leaving Talbothays in Chapter 25 'the sunshine of the morning went out at a stroke'. Angel in Chapter 23 describes Tess as being 'like an undulating billow warmed by the sun', and so on. This symbolism works out neatly with the sacrifice of Tess at Stonehenge brought about by Tess's worship of him and by Angel's rejection of her and his damaging remark about Alec, 'If he were dead it might be different', but there seems no other obvious reason why he should be associated with the sun. Sadly, our final judgement on Angel must be that at the moment of crisis he failed to be true to his beliefs, and like Othello, threw away 'a pearl richer than all his tribe'. It is a successful piece of characterisation made the more so by Hardy's obviously emotional involvement with the man who destroyed his beautiful Tess.

Tess's parents, *Jack and Joan Durbeyfield*, play a significant part in the novel even if for long periods they are missing from the scene. They have, by heredity, influenced Tess's character. In Chapter 37 Hardy writes 'Pride, too, entered into her submission – which perhaps was a symptom of that reckless acquiescence in chance too apparent in the whole d'Urberville family.' We remember here her father's pride in being a d'Urberville, a descendant of a noble and proud family, and his refusal to allow the vicar to come into the house to baptise Tess's dying baby. Jack's character is quickly drawn in the very first chapter. He drinks too much, and his pride, stupidity and fecklessness are revealed in his reaction to the information he receives about his ancestors. In spite of being chronically poor he orders a carriage, and rum, and behaves as if he had inherited money from his ancestors, not just some of what were probably their worst faults. There is something comic about the first chapter but it contains within it the seeds of the tragedy. We feel more sympathy for Tess because she remains loyal to her shiftless, irresponsible father regardless of his weaknesses. A thoroughly bad parent, he even manages to die at the worst possible moment for his daughter!

Joan has the easy-going irresponsibility of her husband, having children without the means to keep them and sharing her husband's love of an alocholic evening at Rolliver's. She is used as a contrast to Tess, and in this contrast Hardy depicts two completely different ways of life. 'Between the mother, with her fast-perishing lumber of superstitions, folk-lore, dialect, and orally transmitted ballads, and the daughter, with her trained National teachings and Standard knowledge under an infinitely Revised Code, there was a gap of two hundred years as ordinarily understood. When they were together the Jacobean and Victorian ages were juxtaposed.' This is an important statement because it partly explains Joan's attitude to her daughter's affairs and her inability to understand Tess's predicament. It is Joan who is mainly responsible for sending her daughter into Alec's clutches at The Slopes. She does nothing to warn Tess of the dangers she faces, assumes that if anything goes wrong Alec will marry her, and when Tess returns pregnant is at first angry, and then accepts the situation with the fatalism of the working-folk who, through suffering, have learnt to accept life's buffets as inevitable. Some might say that her advice to her daughter not to tell Angel of her relationship with Alec was sensible: 'We do not say it'. However, the contrast between the two women is brought out powerfully by their difference in attitudes over the confession. It is difficult to forgive the advantage both mother and father take of Tess, and remarks such as, 'O Tess, what's the use of your playing at marrying gentlemen, if it leaves us like this!' give someone as self-sacrificing as Tess no alternative but to surrender to Alec once again. It is wholly appropriate that her mentioning Sandbourne to Angel leads to his finding Tess and to the deaths of both Alec and her poor daughter. Hardy's attitude to her seems to be ambivalent: he appears to envy her easy-going fatalism and her lack of any sense of guilt, but there is fierce condemnation of her failure as a mother.

There is a whole gallery of *minor characters* – the other members of the Durbeyfield and Clare families, Mercy Chant, Alec's mother, the workers at the dairy – particularly Izz, Marian and Retty, Parson Groby, Mrs Brooks, and others, like the painter of religious texts, who say their few words and are not even named. They all contribute to the picture of rural life in Wessex which Hardy paints so fully. Some, like Angel's brothers and Mercy Chant, seem to be little more than two-dimensional figures created to make a point. Others like *the three dairymaids* are fully life-like – even if perhaps their single-minded devotion to Angel is a little overpowering – and we are given a delightful picture of them at Talbothays. Each is sharply individualised as if Hardy were reminding us that we should not think of farm-folk as being 'personified by the pitiable dummy known as Hodge'. Their love of Tess and their unselfish interest in her well-being make them very sympathetic characters and add to our appreciation of Tess's exceptionally lovable nature. Izz's remark to Angel that 'nobody could love 'ee more than Tess did . . . She would have laid down her life for 'ee' tells us something not only about Tess but also about Izz. With an unusual frankness for the time they are described as passionate girls with strong sexual desires which they know can find no satisfaction with Angel. As Hardy puts it, 'The air of the sleeping-chamber seemed to palpitate with the hopeless passion of the girls. They writhed feverishly under the oppressiveness of an emotion thrust on them by cruel Nature's law.'

Their employer, *Dairyman Crick*, is a splendid piece of characterisation. His bustling energy, his continual good humour and his conscientious involvement with his work make him a living person in whom we can easily believe. In some of his earlier novels Hardy had made use of a rustic chorus of characters who provided much of the humour. In *Tess* we have a number of rustic characters rather than a 'chorus', and such humour as there is in this serious novel comes mainly from the Dairyman. His anecdotes about William Dewy deceiving the bull with his playing of the Nativity Hymn, and Jack Dollop being chased by the mother of the girl he had wronged are very amusing even though they have their more serious side. Hardy knew that what can seem comic to some may be tragic to others. In the Talbothays scenes we learn a great deal about dairy-farming, and Dairyman Crick is an expert at his job. Amusingly, he never touches milk himself but he runs a good dairy and there is the ring of authenticity in such utterances as, 'For Heaven's sake, pop thy hands under the pump, Deb! Upon my soul, if the London folk only knowed of thee and thy slovenly ways, they'd swaller their milk and butter more mincing than they do a'ready.'

In the *Reverend James and Mrs Clare* and their two clerical sons can be seen Hardy's characterisation at its best and worst. He is genuinely interested in the father and mother as sincere evangelical-type Christians whose religion is based upon a love for others – particularly the sinful – and whose selflessness, simplicity and kindness of heart are to be commended. Their anxiety as they await Angel's return from Brazil is touching, and there is much truth in the comment referring to Mrs Clare; 'What woman, indeed, among the faithful adherents of the truth, believes the promises and threats of the Word in the sense in which she believes in her own children, or would not throw her theology to the wind if weighed against their happiness.' Angel's criticism of his father's religious stance is very much that of Hardy himself. Mr Clare's belief in a 'redemptive theolatry' is contrary to the humanistic belief of both Angel and Hardy, but there is no doubting the respect felt for the vicar by his creator. What criticism there is of him is gentle and sympathetic, in stark contrast to the criticism of the brothers who exist to do little more than give Hardy an opportunity of pouring out his contempt for a couple of rigid, snobbish, smug, reactionary dogmatists. Such touches as that of the two brothers insisting that they should push on with their walk in order to 'get through another chapter of *A Counterblast to Agnosticism* before we turn in' are so contrived, and the brothers contribute so little to the actual story, that it is difficult to believe in them. Their inclusion may be regarded as an artistic flaw designed to do little more than give Hardy a chance to vent his disgust at what he sees as worst in the religious Establishment of his time.

Finally, it is worth looking at some of the unnamed characters who play their part in the story. The writer of biblical graffiti who paints lurid warnings to the wicked is a brief but interesting little character sketch based upon a type of person who really existed at that time. There is something grimly real, too, about the engineman who tends the 'red tyrant' on which Tess is to suffer when the threshing takes place at Flintcomb-Ash Farm. He is 'a dark motionless body' who serves 'fire and water' and speaks with 'a strange northern accent'. He, like Alec, is a 'foreigner', an outsider, and his lack of any human contact with the 'natives' is significant because he and his machine represent the forces which are to destroy the old ways of farming. His concentration on his engine and his indifference to whether his environment be 'corn, straw, or chaos' powerfully convey the new attitudes which are coming in with the new farming. Such characters add to the richness of texture of the novel.

5.3 NATURE IN THE NOVEL

The word 'nature' is capable of several different meanings and of some imprecision. One dictionary definition is 'the power that creates and regulates the world'. Hardy certainly sees nature as a powerful force, the life-force which pervades all living creatures and drives them to reproduce themselves so that their species may survive. In *Tess* he emphasises that in natural terms there was nothing sinful in Tess's relationship with Alec. Sin is a concept unknown to nature. Although Hardy sees nature as essentially impersonal and neutral, he cannot resist the tendency we all have to endow the force with human characteristics. Thus we read of 'cruel Nature's law' where the personification is made obvious by the use of a capital 'N'. Tess and Angel are brought together 'under an irresistible law', and the milkmaids 'writhe feverishly under the oppressiveness of an emotion thrust on them by cruel Nature's law'. Hardy makes us aware here of the discrepancy between the animal side of our lives with its strong sexual urges and the restraints which are imposed by the way in which society has evolved. There is irony in Angel's vision of Tess as 'a virginal daughter of Nature', as Nature has no regard whatsoever for virginity.

Having been early influenced by Darwin's *Origin of Species* Hardy has no difficulty in seeing men and animals as being related. Thus, in the incident in which Tess wrings the necks of the wounded pheasants, the hunting party which has caused the damage is described as being 'at once so unmannerly and so unchivalrous towards their weaker fellows in Nature's teeming family'. This relationship between men and animals is brought out in the many comparisons of Tess to animals. Her closeness to the cows is obvious, and she is also repeatedly seen by Hardy as a bird. She is 'like a bird caught in a clap-net', 'like a fascinated bird', and of no more consequence than a bird caught 'in a springe'. In other ways, too, she is associated with birds, with the caged bullfinches at Trantridge, in her remark to Angel that 'the sight of a bird in a cage used often to make me cry', and in the way in which on her way to Talbothays 'in every bird's note seemed to lurk a joy', while when she is sad at being reminded of the past 'only a solitary cracked-voice reed-sparrow greeted her from the bushes by the river'.

In these last instances we can see another important way in which nature functions in a Hardy novel. The well-known term 'Mother Nature' and the fact that we are ourselves part of nature can be taken to imply a human relationship capable of several interpretations. Wordsworth concentrated on the benevolent influences of nature and wrote about 'Nature's holy plan', a phrase which Hardy, who knew far more about rural life than Wordsworth ever did, treats with contempt. As we have seen, 'Mother Nature' in *Tess* is cruel in the imposition of her irresistible laws, and uncaring for her children. Basically, she is, of course, not a person at all but a neutral force, which we sometimes see as kind and benevolent, sometimes cruel and destructive. In *Tess* we find it in two sharply contrasting moods, moods all of us have experienced. At Talbothays in the spring and summer we have what might almost be Wordsworthian nature. The sweet birds sing, the sun shines, flowers and grass grow luxuriantly, the milk from the cows oozes forth and falls in drops to the ground. This is nature at its most luscious and kindly, its most beautiful and generous, and this idyllic scene exquisitely complements the picture of Angel and Tess meeting and falling in love. Their love should be part of the whole natural generative process, and in the fact that it is not to be so lies the pity of it.

As winter comes – and Hardy uses the seasons to build up the required mood – even Talbothays loses its warmth and charm. The marriage takes place and Tess is rejected. Then the married couple call at the dairy before their parting and we see very distinctly how Hardy emphasises the change which has taken place in the words, 'The gold of the summer picture was now gray, the colours mean, the rich soil mud, and the river cold.'

The cold of the winter is the coldness in Tess's life, and Flintcomb-Ash is created by Hardy to reflect that coldness. It is a starve-acre place of harsh labouring jobs such as swede-grubbing in large, flint-covered fields, and after a 'season of congealed dampness came a spell of dry frost', followed by a moisture which 'chilled the eyeballs' and 'penetrated to their skeletons'. Nature here becomes a participant in the story, influencing the reader's response. Our sympathy for Tess, and our sense of her suffering, are made the greater by her exposure to Flintcomb-Ash and the arrival of those 'strange birds from behind the North Pole', those 'gaunt spectral creatures with tragical eyes'. I know of no other writer who has used nature so intensely and powerfully.

Finally, of course, there is the use of nature as the background to the story. Hardy makes us intimately acquainted with three areas of Wessex – the Vale of Blackmoor where Tess was born, the Valley of the Great Dairies where she falls in love with Angel, and Flintcomb-Ash where, rejected and oppressed, she falls again into the clutches of Alec. Each of these three areas is described in such detail that it adds greatly to the impact and richness of the novel. The tragedy of Tess is acted out against a living and detailed background – which at times becomes a foreground – of country life. Better than any history book Hardy's novel describes what it was like to work as a binder of sheaves, as a milker, as a swede-grubber and slicer, as a reed-drawer, and at the threshing of the wheat. Here is country life as it really was lived at that particular moment of time. But the life of the country is threatened by the reaping machine and the threshing machine, and nature itself is on the defensive. One of the most striking images in the book occurs in Chapter 30 where Angel (the outsider) and Tess (the field-woman) take the milk to the station. 'Modern life,' we are told, 'stretched out its steam feeler to this point three or four times a day, touched the native existences, and quickly withdrew its feeler again.' And then we read 'The light of the engine flashed for a second upon Tess Durbeyfield's figure, motionless under the great holly tree.' It is a moment which symbolises unforgettably the impact of the new on the old. It is as if Tess, symbol of an agricultural life which is already doomed by the Industrial Revolution, hangs from the tree as an indication that the way of life which she represents will soon be as dead as she herself will be eventually when she hangs from the gallows-tree.

6 SPECIMEN PASSAGE AND COMMENTARY

From Chapter 19:

It was a typical summer evening in June, the atmosphere being in such delicate equilibrium and so transmissive that inanimate objects seemed endowed with two or three senses, if not five. There was no distinction between the near and the far, and an auditor felt close to everything within the horizon. The soundlessness impressed her as a positive entity rather than as the mere negation of noise. It was broken by the strumming of strings.

Tess had heard those notes in the attic above her head. Dim, flattened, constrained by their confinement, they had never appealed to her as now, when they wandered in the still air with a stark quality like that of nudity. To speak absolutely, both instrument and execution were poor; but the relative is all, and as she listened Tess, like a fascinated bird, could not leave the spot. Far from leaving she drew up towards the performer, keeping behind the hedge that he might not guess her presence.

The outskirt of the garden in which Tess found herself had been left uncultivated for some years, and was now damp and rank with juicy grass which sent up mists of pollen at a touch; and with tall blooming weeds emitting offensive smells – weeds whose red and yellow and purple hues formed a polychrome as dazzling as that of cultivated flowers. She went stealthily as a cat through this profusion of growth, gathering cuckoo-spittle on her skirts, cracking snails that were underfoot, staining her hands with thistle-milk and slug-slime, and rubbing off upon her naked arms sticky blights which, though snow-white on the apple-tree trunks, made madder stains on her skin; thus she drew quite near to Clare, still unobserved of him.

Tess was conscious of neither time nor space. The exaltation which she had described as being producible at will by gazing at a star, came now without any determination of hers; she undulated upon the thin notes of the second-hand harp, and their harmonies passed like breezes through her, bringing tears into her eyes. The floating pollen seemed to be his notes made visible, and the dampness of the garden the weeping of the garden's sensibility. Though near nightfall, the rank-smelling weed-flowers glowed as if they would not close for intentness, and the waves of colour mixed with the waves of sound.

Hardy, as always, sets his scene carefully. We are told that it is a summer evening in June, the month associated with lovers and midsummer. Angel and Tess have met, become interested in each other, and are ripe for falling in love. The atmosphere is in a state of 'delicate equilibrium' and, remembering his comment in Chapter 13 about 'that moment of evening when the light and the darkness are so evenly balanced that the constraint of day and the suspense of night neutralize each other', we may assume that it is twilight, a time which is again a time associated with love. Hardy is constantly endowing inanimate objects with senses – a tradition that goes back to the ancient Greeks – and here he refers to the way in which the atmosphere conveys the impression of 'inanimate objects . . . endowed with two or three senses . . . '. So magical is the atmosphere that the very silence seems something positive broken only 'by the strumming of strings'.

This introduces us to Angel who is playing his second-hand harp, but, as the story will later show us, he is no harp-strumming angel. The notes of the harp disturb the rural silence just as Angel, the outsider, is to disturb by his presence the milkmaids who fall in love with him. To Tess, the notes have a stark quality 'like that of nudity' and through this we are made aware of the elemental nature of this incident. Hardy, who does not share Tess's admiration for Angel, here interpolates the comment that she is listening to a poor instrument being played by a poor executant, but he qualifies this by the shrewd remark that 'the relative is all'. As so often in the novel, Tess is then compared to a bird which, fascinated, is rooted to the spot. Her vulnerability is brought out in this way.

In the next paragraph Tess's progress through the garden is described as she draws nearer to Angel. The description is extremely poetic but Hardy surprises us by making the garden uncultivated, rank with grass and 'with tall blooming weeds emitting offensive smells'. He seems to be deliberately playing down the romantic aspects of the situation, and it may be that he is associating Tess with uncultivated nature and contrasting her with the educated and seemingly sophisticated Angel. This possibility is strengthened by the comparison of Tess to a cat stealthily making her way 'through this profusion of growth'. The paragraph is full of vivid visual details and colours – '*juicy* grass', '*mists* of pollen', 'red and yellow and purple hues', 'slug-*slime*', 'snow-white', '*madder* stains' – but it is not only our visual sense that is being worked on. We have 'offensive *smells*', the sound of '*cracking* snails' and the tactile feeling of '*sticky* blights'. The word 'madder' is used here by Hardy in its old meaning of 'red' (madder is a plant whose root affords a red dye), but there may also be a punning sense of the wildness of the scene, and the blight which is to affect her relationship with Angel is hinted at in the staining of her hands and in the 'sticky blights' which rub off upon her naked arms, and in doing so change from white (innocence and purity) to red (blood and danger). And folklore regards the colours red and white together as foretelling death.

Hardy had always wanted to be a poet rather than a novelist, and his finest passages of prose are full of poetry. We should notice here the assonance of 'damp and rank', the alliteration of 'slug-slime', 'apple-tree trunks' and 'made madder', and the onomatopœia of 'cracking snails'. There is a pronounced rhythm to many of the sentences, and a powerful sense of symmetry. Thus we have 'gathering . . . cracking . . . staining . . . rubbing'. It is interesting, too, to see how often Hardy uses the ten-syllabled blank verse line:

> and was now damp and rank with juicy grass
> which sent up mists of pollen at a touch
> weeds whose red and yellow and purple hues
> gathering cuckoo-spittle on her skirts

There is a deep underlying sense of eroticism about this paragraph. Pollen is, of course, the fertilising powder formed in the anthers of flowers, and we may remember that in the orgiastic scene at the dance at Chaseborough the 'floating fusty *débris* of peat and hay, mixed with the perspiration and warmth of the dancers' formed 'together a sort of vegeto-human pollen'. Sensuous and sensual words like 'juicy' and 'sticky' add to this impression, and we are made strongly aware of Tess's physical presence, of the cuckoo-spittle on her skirts, of her hands, her naked arms and her skin. Some may think that sexual attraction is far more powerfully conveyed in this poetic and imaginative way than by the crude explicitness found in many novels of today.

In the next paragraph the floating pollen is described as seeming to be Angel's notes made visible, and we have here another sexual image. The effect on Tess of Angel's playing of the harp is to bring tears to her eyes, and the description of her undulating upon the notes of the harp echoes the description of Alec's horse in Chapter 8, where in another scene studded with sexual imagery the mare rises and falls in undulations. Tess's feelings for Angel become a mixture of the physical and the spiritual, and a blend of perfect love. A mood of exaltation comes to her and she shares the intentness of the 'rank-smelling weed-flowers' which glow in the twilight. The paragraph ends with a twelve-syllabled sentence divided into two six syllable units of sound: 'and the waves of colour/mixed with the waves of sound', Tess being identified with the colour, Angel with the sound.

There is a remarkable beauty and originality about the writing of this passage as it uses with an intense visionary power the vivid details of the external scene to portray Tess's inner state of feeling. So dense is the writing that it reminds one of the blank verse of Shakespeare's last plays where it is as if the words become heavily charged with a complex of meanings and feelings. This is great prose and all the more remarkable in that it anticipates by many years developments in the writing of fiction which were to come in the twentieth century.

7 CRITICAL RECEPTION

An idea of the immediate response to the publication of *Tess* was given earlier (see page 5). It was both viciously attacked and stoutly defended, and Hardy, who like almost all writers was sensitive about the reception of his books, was very much hurt by the stridency of some of the reviewers. However, it was not long before critical comment became largely favourable. Such opposition as there was became based far less upon Hardy's attitude to the Church and to sexual morals, and rather more upon his style, his so-called 'pessimism', his authorial intrusions, and his alleged philosophical inconsistencies. Not that the Establishment found it easy to forgive him. As late as 1943 it was possible for an Archbishop of Canterbury to say, 'Hardy's *Tess of the d'Urbervilles* is one of the worst books ever written.'

Public demand for the novel became so big that 100 000 copies of a cheap paperback edition were sold in 1900-1. It was also translated into several European languages, and in our century it has been adapted for the stage on several occasions and has twice been made into a film. In 1906 it was performed in Naples as an opera, (the first performance being marked, coincidentally, by an eruption of Mount Vesuvius). It has been an inspiration to other creative artists.

Of the very many twentieth-century critics who have written about *Tess*, D. H. Lawrence in his *Study of Thomas Hardy* (1914) is possibly the most remarkable. It is, as one might expect, more about Lawrence himself and his ideas than about Hardy, but it has some interesting and unusual insights into the novel:

> It is not Angel Clare's fault that he cannot come to Tess when he finds that she has, in his own words, been defiled. It is the result of generations of ultra-Christian training, which has left in him an inherent aversion to the female, and in all in himself which pertained to the female. What he, in his Christian sense, conceived of

as Woman, was only the servant and attendant and administering
spirit to the male. He had no idea that there was such a thing as
positive Woman, as the Female, another great living principle counter-
balancing his own male principle. He conceived of the world as
consisting of the One, the Male Principle ... There seems to be in
d'Urberville an inherent antagonism to any progression in himself.
Yet he seeks with all his power for the source of stimulus in woman.
He takes the deep impulse from the female. In this he is exceptional ... Alec d'Urberville could reach some of the real sources
of the female in a woman, and draw from them. And, as a woman
instinctively knows, such men are rare. Therefore they have a power
over a woman. They draw from the depth of her being.

We may not always agree with Lawrence but he makes us think, and
although he is critical of the way in which Hardy's characters are usually
overcome by society he had no doubt of his greatness as a novelist.

It is possible to quote from only a few of the very many articles and
books which have been written on *Tess* since Lawrence's *Study* but here
are four examples which will give some idea of the very many different
aspects of critical comment:

> There is just enough plot loosely to thread together the several
> episodes that comprise the book, yet surely it is not here that one
> looks for Hardy's achievement. *Tess of the d'Urbervilles* can, in fact,
> profitably be regarded as a fiction in the line of *Pilgrim's Progress* ...
> for its structure is that of a journey in which each place of rest
> becomes a test for the soul and the function of plot is largely to
> serve as an agency for transporting the central figure from one
> point to another. *Tess* is clearly not an allegory and no one in his
> senses would wish that it were, but its pattern of narrative has
> something in common with, even if it does not directly draw upon,
> Bunyan's fiction. There are four sections or panels of representation:
> Tess at home and with Alec; Tess at Talbothays and with Angel;
> Tess at Flintcomb-Ash and again with Alec: Tess briefly happy with
> Angel and then in her concluding apotheosis at Stonehenge. None
> of these panels is quite self-sufficient, since narrative tension ac-
> cumulates from part to part; but each has a distinctiveness of place,
> action and tone which makes it profitable to think of the novel as
> episodic. One is reminded of a medieval painting divided into panels,
> each telling a part of a story and forming a progress in martyrdom.
> The martyrdom is that of Tess, upon whom everything rests and all
> value depends. (Irving Howe, *Thomas Hardy*, 1985.)

For an artist as visually sensitive as Hardy, colour is of the first importance and significance, and there is one colour which literally catches the eye, and is meant to catch it, throughout the book. This colour is red, the colour of blood, which is associated with Tess from first to last . . . She is full of it, she spills it, she loses it . . . The first time we (and Angel) see Tess, in the May dance with the other girls, she stands out. How? They are all white except that Tess "wore a red ribbon in her hair, and was the only one of the white company who could boast of such a pronounced adornment". Tess is marked, even from the happy valley of her birth and child-hood . . . This patterning of red and white is often visible in the background of the book. For instance "The ripe hue of the red and dun kine absorbed the evening sunlight, which the white-coated animals returned to the eye in rays almost dazzling, even at the distant elevation on which she stood." This dark red and dazzling white is something seen, it is something there; it is an effect on the retina, it is a configuration of matter. In looking at this landscape Tess in fact is seeing the elemental mixture which conditions her own existence. (Tony Tanner, essay in *The Critical Quarterly*, Autumn 1968.)

The poetic vision gives supreme importance to Tess's inner, unique experience of the world through her sensations and emotions; unusually detailed for Hardy. She is also defined by the poetry of her work. Even the harsh work at Flintcomb-Ash borrows poetic beauty from the transformations of frost and snow and the tragic evocations of the Northern birds who share and universalize Tess's will to live. The differing kinds of work take their special rhythm from the rhythms of her life, sensitively realised in narrative and speech structure. The rhythms of Talbothays, slow and contem-plative or simple and passionate, reflecting her sweep to maturity with its hesitations, crises, reprieves and rallies, build up a very different emotional response from the monotonous, consonantal rhythm of mechanical work at Flintcomb-Ash, or the deadness of shocked existence, detail after dragging detail in flat bald sentences at Wellbridge Manor. Hardy's dialogue is not always inspired: perhaps even Angel would hardly have met the greatest crisis of his life with "My God – how can forgiveness meet such a grotesque – pre-stidigitation as that!" – but Tess's stupefied simplicity in the quarrel, her bare statements of truth . . . catch the intimate cadences of a noble and passionate woman. (Jean Brooks, *Thomas Hardy: The Poetic Structure*, 1971.)

In the last, notorious paragraph of the novel all the resonances of the novel are heard:

> 'Justice' was done, and the President of the Immortals, in Aeschylean phrase, had ended his sport with Tess. And the d'Urberville knights and dames slept on in their tombs unknowing. The two speechless gazers bent themselves down to the earth, as if in prayer, and remained thus a long time, absolutely motionless: the flag continued to wave silently. As soon as they had strength they arose, joined hands again, and went on.

How often the opening sentence of that paragraph has been quoted in isolation, and made to serve as 'the conclusion' to the novel, whereas Hardy, true to his practice, makes his conclusion multiple in emphasis. The first sentence is a sombre acknowledgement of forces in the world over which we would seem to have little or no control. It is followed by a sentence which shifts from metaphysics to history, proclaiming the serene indifference of the past to the present. These two sentences are followed by two others which indicate contrary possibilities. We see an intimation of human resilience in 'the speechless gazers' who seek in the earth itself, in the conditions of man's terrestrial existence, notwithstanding his mutability, hope and not despair. In the last sentence hope turns into strength, strength to affirm the human bond and to give direction to action, 'they . . . joined hands again, and went on'. It is a sentence which recalls, in its rhythm, the sadness – and the resolution – present in the final lines of *Paradise Lost*:

> They hand in hand with wandring steps and slow,
> Through *Eden* took their solitarie way.

It would be as foolish to isolate Hardy's last sentence and see the final emphasis of the novel to lie there as it would be to isolate the first. For him, it is the four sentences taken together which constitute a human truth, by catching in various lights our condition, flux followed by reflux, the fall by the rally; it is this sense of continuous movement which suggests that the fiction which records it should be described as 'a series of seemings'. (Ian Gregor, *The Great Web*, 1974.)

REVISION QUESTIONS

1. Discuss the part played in *Tess* by symbolism.

2. 'The novel involves particular people and places at a specific time; but the events have a significance for all people at any time.' Discuss.

3. What use does Hardy make of colours in *Tess*?

4. Hardy wrote, 'The best tragedy – highest tragedy in short – is that of the worthy encompassed by the inevitable.' To what extent can *Tess*, in the light of this, be regarded as a tragedy?

5. What do you regard as the function of the natural background in *Tess*?

6. 'In reading a Hardy novel the reader feels at once that a craftsman is in charge.' What evidence have you found in *Tess* to support this statement?

7. Discuss the view that *Tess* is spoilt by Hardy's authorial comments.

8. 'The good little Thomas Hardy has scored a great success with *Tess of the d'Urbervilles* which is chock-full of faults and falsity, and yet has a singular charm' (Henry James). Consider the novel in the light of this comment.

9. 'My art is to intensify the expression of things . . . so that the heart and inner meaning is made vividly visible.' Consider Hardy's statement in relation to *Tess*.

10. To what extent is Tess responsible for what happens to her?

FURTHER READING

Texts
There are several annotated texts available, of which the best are the New Wessex (Macmillan), Everyman Library (Dent), and the Penguin English Library editions. Simon Gatrell's Clarendon Edition (OUP) provides a fascinating insight into how Hardy shaped his text.

Biography
The Life of Thomas Hardy by Thomas Hardy, ed. Michael Millgate (Macmillan, 1985), is invaluable and contains many observations by Hardy on his career as a novelist.

Another good biography is *Thomas Hardy: A Biography* by Michael Millgate (OUP, 1982)

Critical Works
Brooks, Jean, *Thomas Hardy: The Poetic Structure* (Elek, 1971)
Cecil, David, *Hardy the Novelist* (Constable, 1943)
Gregor, Ian, *The Great Web* (Faber, 1974)
Howe, Irving, *Thomas Hardy* (Macmillan, 1985)
Millgate, Michael, *Thomas Hardy: His Career as a Novelist* (Bodley Head 1971)
Morrell, Roy, *Thomas Hardy; The Will and the Way* (OUP, 1965)
Smith, Anne (ed.), *The Novels of Thomas Hardy* (Vision, 1979)
Draper, R. P., *A Casebook: Hardy, The Tragic Novels* (Macmillan, 1975)
Laird, J. T., *The Shaping of 'Tess of the d'Urbervilles'* (OUP, 1975)